W9-AYF-457

Ready® Common Core

1 Mathematics INSTRUCTION

3 tens + ? tens = 8 tens

Associate Vice President: Renee Gardner
Editorial Director: Cindy Tripp
Associate Editorial Director: Thomas Super
Project Manager: Jillian McCarthy
Editors: Danielle Curran, Pam Halloran, Kathy Kellman,
Theresa MacVicar, Dawn Nuttall, Lauren Van Wart
Cover Design: Matt Pollock
Cover Illustrator: O'Lamar Gibson
Book Design: Mark Nodland, Timothy Theriault

ISBN 978-1-4957-2003-1
©2017–Curriculum Associates, LLC
North Billerica, MA 01862

BTS19
15 14

Table of Contents

Standards in boldface are the focus standards that address major lesson content.

Table of Contents continued

Standards in boldface are the focus standards that address major lesson content.

Standards in boldface are the focus standards that address major lesson content.

Table of Contents continued

Standards in boldface are the focus standards that address major lesson content.

Lee wants to share some stickers. He wants some stickers for his notebook. What math questions could Lee ask about the stickers?

In this unit you will learn ways to add and subtract. Then you will be able to solve problems like Lee's!

✓ Self Check

Check off the skills you know now. Then see how many more you can check off after each lesson!

I can:	Before this unit	After this unit
count on to add.	☐	☐
count on to subtract.	☐	☐
solve addition and subtraction word problems.	☐	☐
use addition sentences to write subtraction sentences.	☐	☐
find missing addends.	☐	☐
subtract to compare.	☐	☐

G | **Explore It**

There are 4 boys and 2 girls in the group.

How many children are in the group?

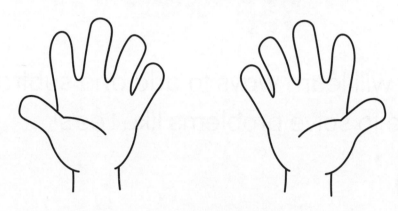

_____ **children**

There are 4 boys and 3 girls in the group.

How many children are in the group?

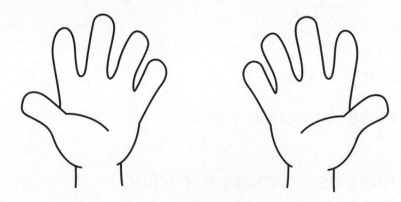

_____ **children**

▶▶ **Try It**

There are 5 girls and 3 boys on a team.
How many children are on the team?

There are _____ children on the team.

Count On to Add

A team has 5 girls and 3 boys.
How many children are on the team in all?

Model It Find 5 + 3. ••••••••••••••••••••••••••••••••••••••

One part shows girls. One part shows boys.
Count on from 5 to **add** girls and boys.

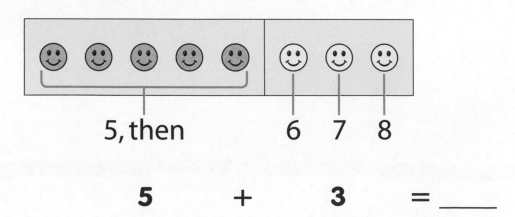

5, then   6 7 8

5   +   3   = _____

Learn Together
Count On to Add

6 blocks are yellow. 2 blocks are red.
How many blocks in all?
How do you know?

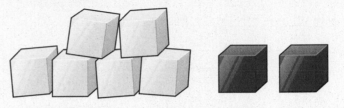

 **Model It** Find 6 + 2.

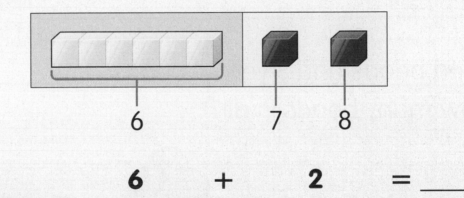

6   7   8

6   **+**   **2**   = _____

Talk About It **What is wrong?**

6 blocks are yellow. 3 blocks are red.
How many blocks in all?
What's wrong?

1, then   2,   3,   4

▶ Show the right way.   ____, then ____, ____, ____

6   **+**   **3**   = _____

Practice Together
Count On to Add

5 red markers and 3 blue markers.
How many markers in all?

$5 + 3 =$ ___8___

5
red

6 7 8

---

1 6 red beads and 3 yellow beads.
How many beads in all?

$6 + 3 =$ ____

---

2 6 red blocks and 2 blue blocks.
How many blocks in all?

$6 + 2 =$ ____

6

Count On to Add

3 5 big balls and 3 small balls.
How many balls in all?

5 + 3 = ____
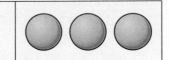

4 1 bee and 7 ants.
How many bugs in all?

1 + 7 = ____

5 6 triangles and 2 squares.
How many shapes in all?

____ = 6 + 2

 **Explore It**

5 children are playing ball. 3 children leave.
How many children are still playing ball?

_____ – _____ = _____   _____ + _____ = _____

6 children are playing ball. 4 children leave.
How many children are still playing ball?

6 – _____ = _____   _____ + _____ = _____

©Curriculum Associates, LLC   Copying is not permitted.

 **Try It**

8 children are playing ball. 5 children leave.
How many children are still playing ball?

8 − ___ = ___   ___ + ___ = ___

6 children are playing ball. 3 children leave.
How many children are still playing ball?

6 − ___ = ___   ___ + ___ = ___

Count On to Subtract

6 children play ball. 4 go home early.
How many children are left?

Model It Find 6 − 4. ●

Start with the number of children who leave.

Start at 4.   Count on to 6.
                              Count on ___2___.

6 − 4 = ___

Learn Together
Count On to Subtract

There are 7 bikes. 4 are red.
The rest are black.

How many are black?
How can you find out?

Model It **Find 7 − 4.** •

Start at 4.   Count on to 7.

1 2 3 ④ 5 6 7 8 9 10

$7 - 4 =$ _____ $4 +$ _____ $= 7$

Talk About It **Who is right? How do you know?** • • • • • • • • • •

There are 8 children. 5 are boys. How many are girls?

Buzz: Boom:

5 6 7 8   5   6 7 8

$8 - 5 = 4$ $8 - 5 = 3$

Practice Together
Count On to Subtract

Ali has 7 markers. Some are blue.

5 are red.

How many are blue?

$7 - 5 = ?$

5 + __2__ **= 7**

5 red

6 7

---

1 There are 8 cups. 5 are big. The rest are small.

How many are small?

8 − 5 = _____   **8 =** _____ **+ 5**

---

2 There are 9 balloons. 6 balloons pop.

How many balloons are left?

1 2 3 4 5 ⑥ 7 8 9 10

9 − 6 = _____   **6 + 3 =** _____

Count On to Subtract

3 Jen has 8 buttons. 6 are square.

The rest are round. How many buttons are round?

8 − 6 = _____   6 + _____ = 8

4 6 fish are in the weeds. 3 swim away.

How many are left?

1	2	3	4	5	6	7	8	9	10

6 − 3 = _____   6 = 3 + _____

5 6 flowers are in a vase.

5 flowers are short.

The rest are tall.

How many flowers are tall?

6 − 5 = _____   5 + _____ = 6

G Explore It

There is room for 5 children.

3 children are already sitting.

How many more will fit?

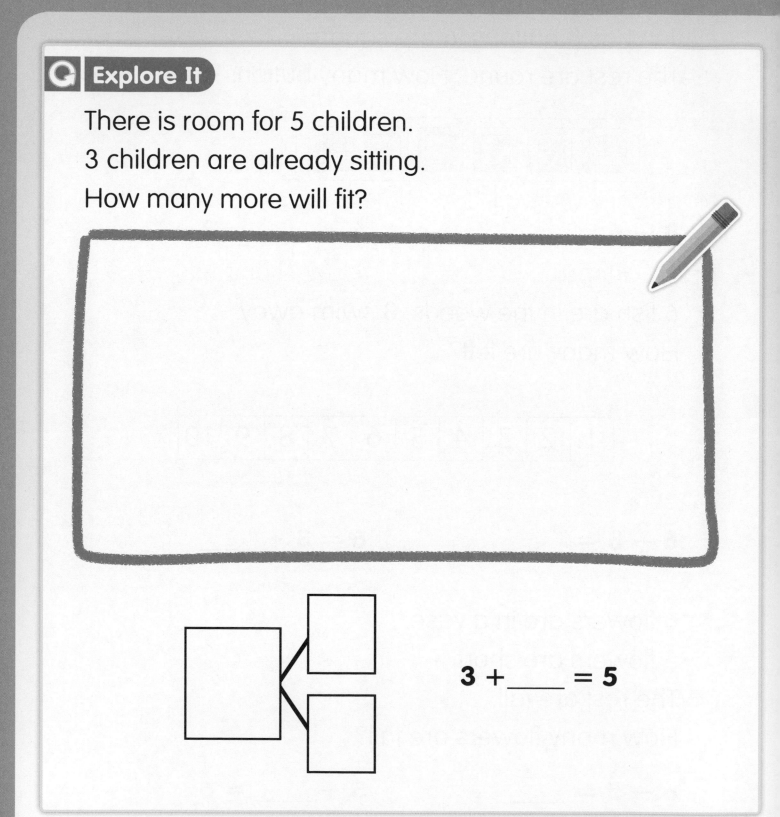

$$3 + \underline{} = 5$$

 **Try It**

1 animal was drinking from a pool.

Later, more animals came. Now there are 4 animals.

How many animals came later?

First: 1 animal

Now: 4 animals

____ + ____ = ____

Add and Subtract in Word Problems

3 children are sitting.

More children sit down.

Now there are 5 children.

How many more children sit down?

Model It   **Find 3 + ____ = 5.** •••••••••••••••••••••••••••••••••••

Start with 3. Count on.

How many more make 5?

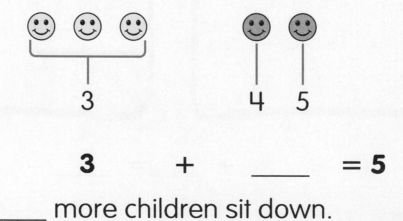

3   4   5

3   **+**   **____**   **= 5**

____ more children sit down.

Add and Subtract in Word Problems

Jan has 6 pencils.
She gives some away.
Now she has 5 pencils.
How many does she give away?

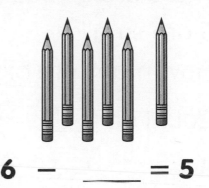

$$6 - \underline{\quad} = 5$$

Model It Find $6 - \underline{\quad} = 5$.

Start with 5. How many more makes 6?

$$5 + \underline{\quad} = 6$$

$$6 - \underline{\quad} = 5$$

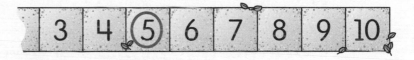

Jan gives away ____ pencil(s).

Talk About It Who is right? How do you know?

There are 8 pencils.
4 are yellow. The rest are blue.
How many are blue?

Buzz: $4 + 8 = ?$ Boom: $4 + ? = 8$

Practice Together
Add and Subtract in Word Problems

There are 8 frogs. Some are big.

5 are small.

How many are big?

Count on __3__ .

8 − __3__ **= 5**

__3__ frogs are big.

1 Greg has 8 toys. He puts some away.

Now there are 6 toys.

How many toys are put away?

8 − __2__ **= 6**

__2__ toys are put away.

2 There are 7 balls. 5 are soccer balls.

The rest are kickballs.

How many kickballs are there?

__2__ **+ 5 = 7**

There are __2__ kickballs.

Add and Subtract in Word Problems

3 Emma has 3 beads. She gets more beads.

Now she has 6.

How many new beads does she get?

3 + ___3___ **= 6**

Emma gets ___3___ new beads.

---

4 9 kites are flying. Some fall.

Now there are 7 kites.

How many kites fall?

9 − ___2___ **= 7**

___2___ kites fall.

---

5 Jimmy picks 7 peppers. 5 are green.

The rest are red.

How many peppers are red?

5 + ___2___ **= 7**

___2___ peppers are red.

G | **Explore It**

8 rabbits are eating lunch.

Some rabbits eat carrots and some eat lettuce.

5 rabbits eat carrots. How many rabbits eat lettuce?

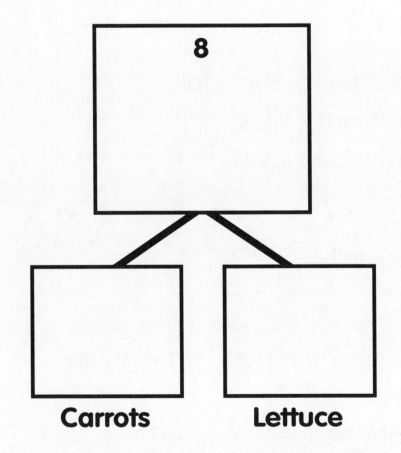

____ + ____ = ____   ____ – ____ = ____

____ + ____ = ____   ____ – ____ = ____

 **Try It**

7 mice are eating lunch.

Some mice eat nuts and some eat seeds.

3 mice eat nuts. How many mice eat seeds?

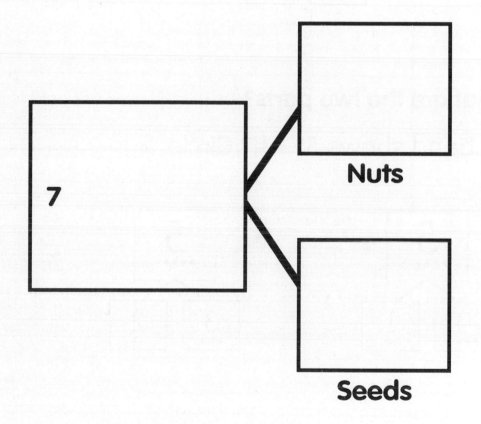

____ = ____ + ____   ____ = ____ − ____

____ = ____ + ____   ____ = ____ − ____

Introduction **Lesson 4**   **21**

Understand Missing Addends

> How can adding help you subtract?

$5 - 4 = ?$

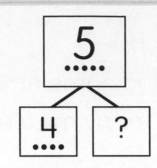

Think   **What are the two parts?** ·

Which number bond shows $5 - 4$? Circle.

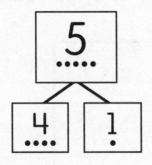   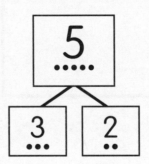

Talk About It ·

What addition sentence helps you find $5 - 4$?

Explore Together
Understand Missing Addends

 Find 7 − 3.

Use 7 counters. Keep 3. → Put the rest in a cup. → Write the answer.

$3 + \underline{4} = 7$

$7 - 3 = \underline{4}$

---

1 **Find 7 − 5.**

Draw and write.

$5 + \underline{} = 7$

$7 - 5 = \underline{}$

2 **Find 7 − 4.**

Draw and write.

$4 + \underline{} = 7$

$7 - 4 = \underline{}$

💬 **Talk About It** •

How can you add to find 6 − 4?

Guided Instruction **Lesson 4**   **23**

Understand Missing Addends

3 **Show** Write a subtraction sentence.
Then write an addition sentence.

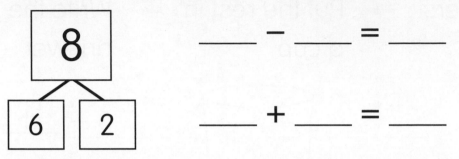

___ − ___ = ___

___ + ___ = ___

4 **Reason** There are 8 cats. 5 are black.
The rest are gray. How many are gray?

Show how you solve.

5 **Explain** There are 5 beads. 4 are on the table.
The rest are in a cup.

▸ Buzz says there are 9 beads in the cup.
▸ Do you agree? Why? Why not?

Understand Missing Addends

6 **Think about missing addends.**

A: Color some triangles red and some blue.
Complete the number bond. Write a subtraction
and an addition sentence.

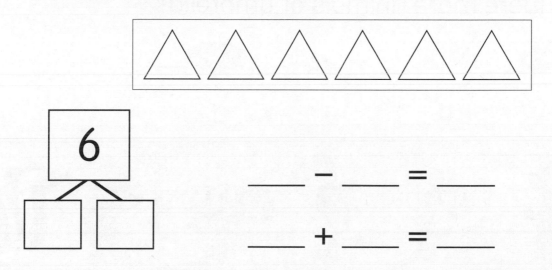

___ − ___ = ___

___ + ___ = ___

B: Color a different number of triangles red and blue.
Complete the number bond. Write a subtraction
and an addition sentence.

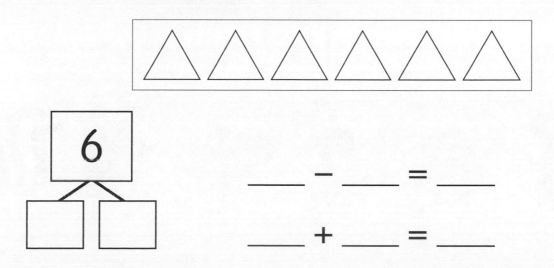

___ − ___ = ___

___ + ___ = ___

G **Explore It**

There are 4 umbrellas. There are 6 animals.
Are there more animals or umbrellas?

There are 4 umbrellas. There are 6 animals.
Are there fewer animals or umbrellas?

Subtract to Compare in Word Problems

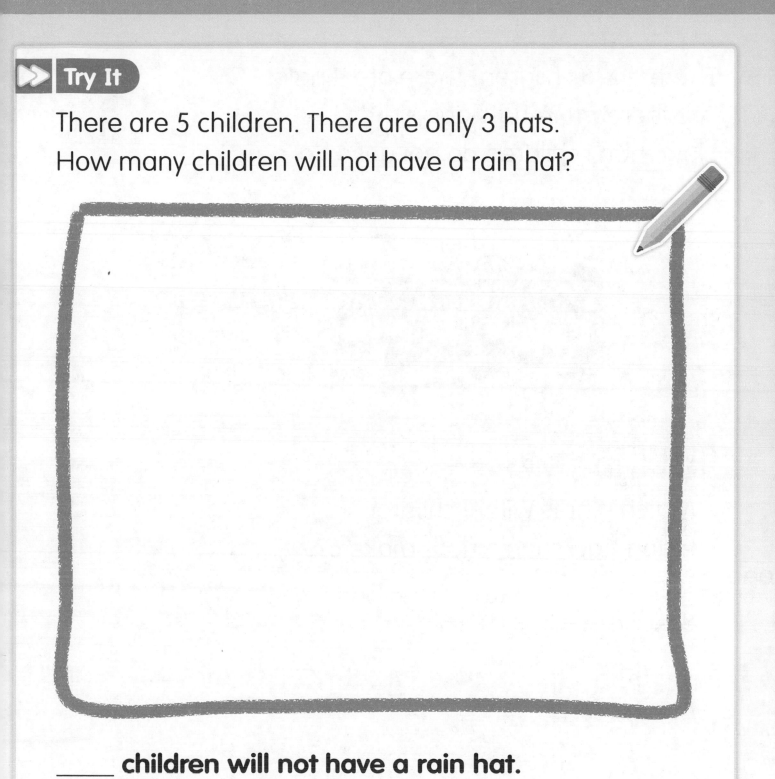

>> **Try It**

There are 5 children. There are only 3 hats.
How many children will not have a rain hat?

____ **children will not have a rain hat.**

Subtract to Compare in Word Problems

There are 6 children. There are 4 hats.

Are there **more** hats or children?

How many children do not get a hat?

⊞ Model It Find 6 − 4. •

Match 4 hats with 4 children.

4 and how many more make 6?

6 − 4 = ____

_____ children do not get a hat.

Subtract to Compare in Word Problems

There are 5 pieces of cheese and 8 mice.
Are there **fewer** mice or pieces of cheese?
How many mice do not get cheese?

▦ Model It Find 8 − 5. •

Start with 5.

5 and how many more make 8?

8 − 5 = ____

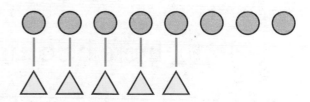

💬 Talk About It Who is right? How do you know? • • • • • • • • • •

How many fewer sticks than skates
are there?

Buzz says there are 3 fewer sticks.
Boom says there is 1 fewer stick.

Subtract to Compare in Word Problems

Nan sees 6 birds. Cam sees 9 birds.
How many fewer birds does Nan see?

9 − 6 = __3__

Nan sees __3__ fewer birds.

---

1   4 red markers and 7 blue markers.
How many more blue markers are there?

7 − 4 = ____

____ more blue markers

---

2   8 apples and 6 bananas.
How many more apples
are there?

____ more apples

Subtract to Compare in Word Problems

3 Jo has 7 fish. Pat has 6 fish.
How many more fish does Jo have?

7 − ____ = 6

Jo has ____ more fish.

4 7 big shells and 9 small shells.
How many more small shells are there?

9 − ____ = ____

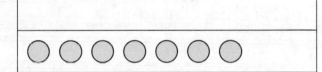

____ more small shells

5 5 chairs and 6 desks.
How many fewer chairs are there?

6 − ____ = ____

____ fewer chair(s)

Solve the problems.

1 8 blocks in all. 6 are red.
Some are blue.
How many are blue?

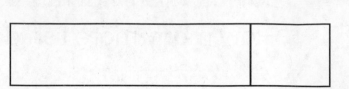

8 − _____ **= 6**

---

2 5 children play. 3 more children come.
How many children in all?

| 1 | 2 | 3 | 4 | 5 | 6 | 7 | 8 | 9 | 10 |

_____ **= 5 + 3**

---

3 **7 − 2 =** _____

4 **6 + 3 =** _____

5 _____ **= 9 − 2**

6 **6 + 1 =** _____

7 6 birds and 3 ants. How many more birds are there than ants?

Draw a picture that shows the problem.
Then write a number sentence.

_____ – _____ = _____

There are _____ more birds than ants.

---

8 9 buttons in all.
7 are square. Some are round.
How many are round?

Complete the number bond.
Write an addition sentence.
Then write a subtraction sentence.

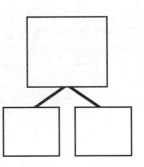

_____ + _____ = _____   _____ – _____ = _____

There are _____ round buttons.

Put It Together

9 **Draw a picture to show an addition story problem.**

Use the numbers 7, 5, and 2.
Tell or write your addition problem.
Write the addition sentence.

_____ + _____ = _____

 Beth wants to draw pictures of some of the flowers. What math questions could Beth ask about the flowers?

In this unit, you will learn different ways to make and add numbers to 10. Then you will be able to solve problems like Beth's.

✓ Self Check

Check off the skills you know now. Then see how many more you can check off after each lesson!

I can:	Before this unit	After this unit
use doubles and doubles plus 1 to add.	☐	☐
find number partners for 6 and 7.	☐	☐
find number partners for 8 and 9.	☐	☐
find number partners for 10.	☐	☐
tell the meaning of the equal sign (=).	☐	☐
tell if a number sentence is true or untrue.	☐	☐
add numbers with totals to 10.	☐	☐

G | **Explore It**

Children line up on both sides of the field.
There are 4 children on each side.
How many children are there?

___ + ___ = ___

One more child joins the group on the left.
Now how many children are there?

___ + ___ + ___ = ___

 **Try It**

Max has 3 red beads and 3 blue beads.

How many beads does Max have?

Then Max finds 1 more red bead.

Now how many beads does Max have in all?

____ + ____ = ____

Max has ____ beads.

____ + ____ + ____ = ____

Now Max has ____ beads in all.

Explore Together
Doubles and Doubles Plus 1

3 players pass a ball.

3 players trap a ball.

How many players in all?

Model It   **Find 3 + 3.** ....

Each addend is 3.

Use **doubles** to find the total.

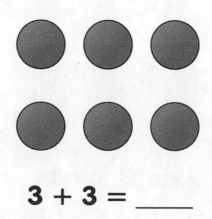

$$3 + 3 = \underline{\quad\quad}$$

Learn Together
Doubles and Doubles Plus 1

3 players on the blue team. 4 players on the red team. How many players in all?

Model It   **Use doubles. Add 1 more.** ....

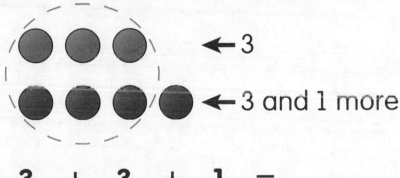

←3

←3 and 1 more

$3 \ + \ 3 \ + \ 1 \ = \ \_\_\_$

$3 \ + \ \ \ \ 4 \ \ \ \ = \ \_\_\_$

Talk About It   **Who is right? How do you know?** ....

Boom wrote: $4 + 4 + 1$.

Buzz wrote: $5 + 5 - 1$.

Doubles and Doubles Plus 1

2 red blocks and 3 blue blocks.
How many blocks in all?

2 + 2 + 1 = _5_

2 +   3   = _5_

← 2

← 2 + 1

---

1 There are 4 balls. 2 are big. The rest are small.
How many balls are small?

2 + ___ = 4

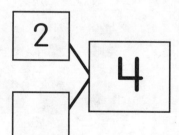

---

2 Jo has 4 pencils. She finds 3 more pencils.
How many pencils does Jo have in all?

3 + 3 + ___ = ___

3 + 4 = ___

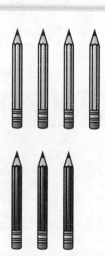

Doubles and Doubles Plus 1

3 2 books and 3 books.
How many books in all?

___ + ___ + ___ = ___

2 + 3 = ___

4 There are 4 birds. More birds join them.
Now there are 8 birds.
How many birds join?

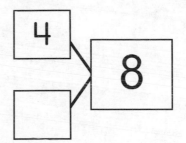

4 + ___ = 8

5 Nick has 5 sun stickers.
He has 5 moon stickers.
How many stickers does Nick have in all?

5 + 5 = ___

 **Explore It**

A domino has 6 dots.

What are some ways to show 6?

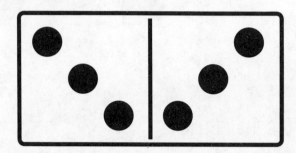

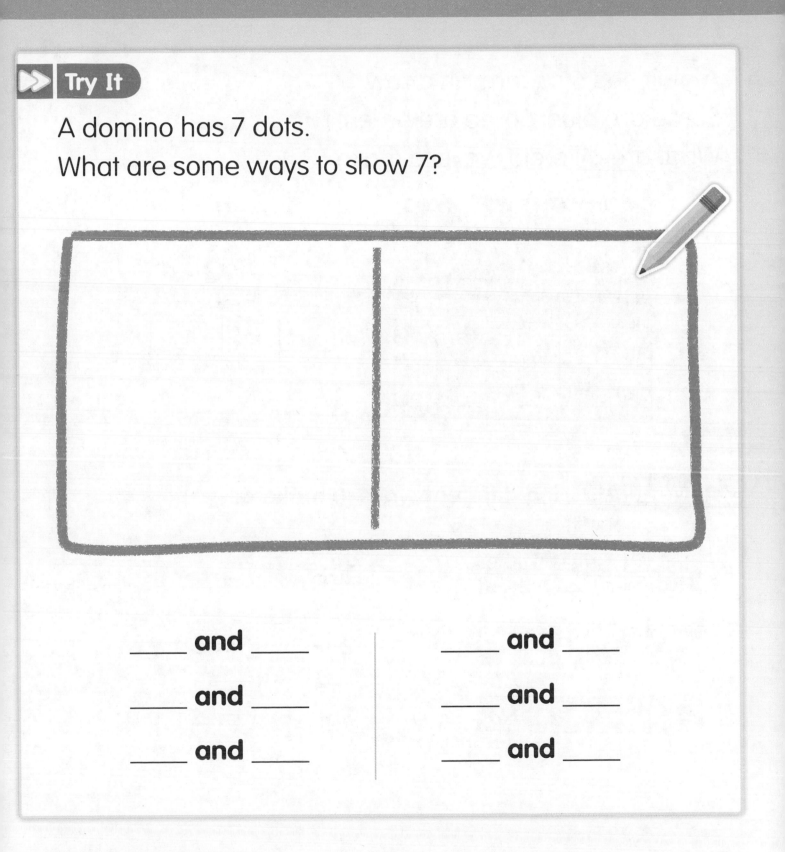

>> **Try It**

A domino has 7 dots.
What are some ways to show 7?

_____ **and** _____   _____ **and** _____

_____ **and** _____   _____ **and** _____

_____ **and** _____   _____ **and** _____

Number Partners for 6 and 7

A quilt has 6 squares in a row.

Some are blue. Some are green.

What are different ways to make 6?

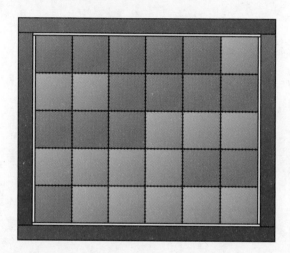

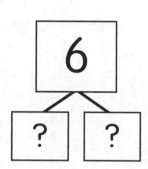

Model It Find different ways to make 6. ·

$1 + \underline{\ 5\ } = 6$

$2 + \underline{\qquad} = 6$

$3 + \underline{\qquad} = 6$

Number Partners for 6 and 7

A painting has 7 circles in a row.
Some are purple. Some are orange.
What are different ways to make 7?

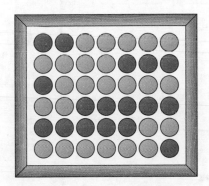

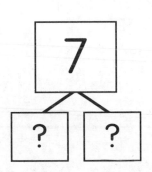

Model It Find different ways to make 7.

 $1 + \_\_\_ = 7$

 $2 + \_\_\_ = 7$

 $3 + \_\_\_ = 7$

Talk About It Who is right? How do you know?

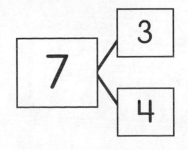

Boom writes: $3 + 4 = 7$.

Buzz writes: $4 = 7 - 3$.

Number Partners for 6 and 7

Write four number sentences.

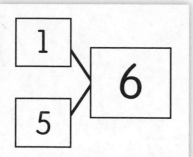

$6 = \underline{\ 1\ } + \underline{\ 5\ }$

$6 = \underline{\ 5\ } + \underline{\ 1\ }$

$6 - \underline{\ 1\ } = \underline{\ 5\ }$

$6 - \underline{\ 5\ } = \underline{\ 1\ }$

1 Complete the number bond.
Write two addition sentences.

3	

7

$7 = \underline{\quad} + \underline{\quad}$

$7 = \underline{\quad} + \underline{\quad}$

2 Complete the number bond.
Write a subtraction sentence.

	3

6

$3 = 6 - \underline{\quad}$

Practice by Myself
Number Partners for 6 and 7

3 Complete the number bond.
Write two subtraction sentences.

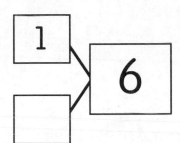

6 – _____ = _____

_____ = 6 – _____

4 Complete the number bond.
Write two addition sentences.

7 = _____ + _____

_____ + _____ = 7

5 Complete the number bond.
Write four number sentences.

_____ + _____ = 7   7 – _____ = _____

7 = _____ + _____   _____ = 7 – _____

Number Partners for 8 and 9

G **Explore It**

There are 2 vans to carry 8 people.

How many people are in each van?

 **Try It**

There are 9 apples. There are 2 apple trees.
Show all the ways the apples could be on the 2 trees.

____ **and** ____   ____ **and** ____

____ **and** ____   ____ **and** ____

____ **and** ____   ____ **and** ____

____ **and** ____   ____ **and** ____

Introduction **Lesson 8**   **49**

Number Partners for 8 and 9

Ed rolls two number cubes.

He adds to get 8.

What are different ways to make 8?

Model It Find different ways to make 8. • • • • • • • • • • • • • • • • • • •

$1 + \underline{} 7 = 8$ $\underline{} + 1 = 8$

$2 + \underline{} 6 = 8$ $\underline{} + 2 = 8$

$3 + \underline{} 5 = 8$ $\underline{} + 3 = 8$

$4 + \underline{} 4 = 8$

Number Partners for 8 and 9

A teacher makes a group of 9 children.
Some are girls. Some are boys.
What are all the ways to make 9?

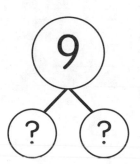

Model It Find different ways to make 9.

 $1 +$ _____ $= 9$ _____ $+ 1 = 9$

 $2 +$ _____ $= 9$ _____ $+ 2 = 9$

 $3 +$ _____ $= 9$ _____ $+ 3 = 9$

 $4 +$ _____ $= 9$ _____ $+ 4 = 9$

Talk About It Do you agree? Why or why not?

Buzz says that 0 and 9
are partners of 9.

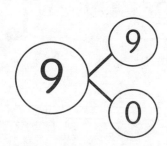

Number Partners for 8 and 9

Write four number sentences.

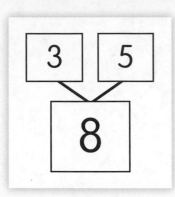

$8 = \underline{3} + \underline{5}$

$8 = \underline{5} + \underline{3}$

$8 - \underline{3} = \underline{5}$

$8 - \underline{5} = \underline{3}$

1 Complete the number bond.
Write two addition sentences.

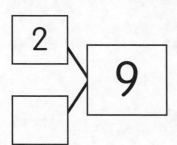

$\underline{} + \underline{} = 9$

$\underline{} + \underline{} = 9$

2 Complete the number bond.
Write two subtraction sentences.

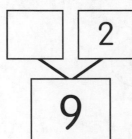

$9 - \underline{} = \underline{}$

$9 - \underline{} = \underline{}$

Number Partners for 8 and 9

3 Complete the number bond.
Write two subtraction sentences.

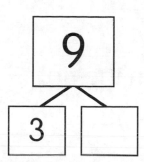

_____ = 9 − _____

9 − _____ = _____

4 Complete the number bond.
Write two addition sentences.

9 = _____ + _____

_____ + _____ = 9

5 Complete the number bond.
Write four number sentences.

___ + ___ = 8   ___ − ___ = 2

8 = ___ + ___   ___ = 8 − ___

Number Partners for 10

Ⓖ Explore It

10 spaceships return home from Earth.

Some land on the left and some land on the right.

How could the spaceships land?

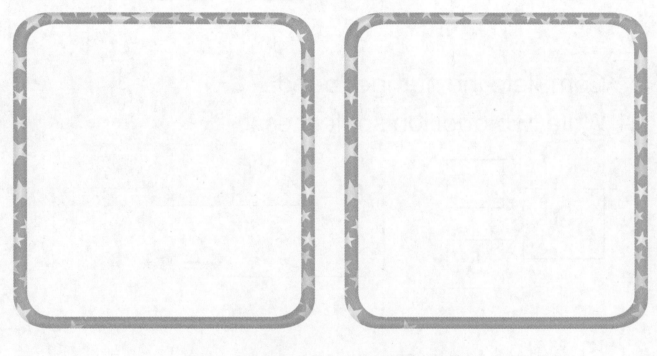

_____ and _____ make 10.

_____ and _____ make 10.

_____ and _____ make 10.

_____ and _____ make 10.

>> **Try It**

Mia needs to show two cards that make 10.
What are five ways she could show 10?

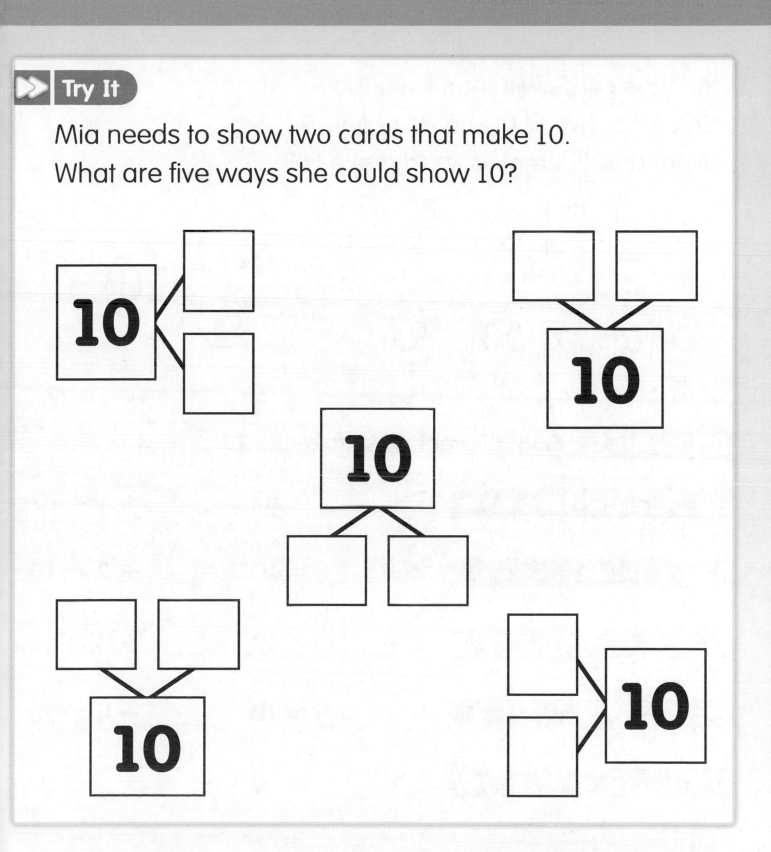

Number Partners for 10

Jen has cards with numbers 1 to 9.
She adds two of the cards to get 10.
What are different ways to make 10?

1   2   3   4   5

6   7   8   9

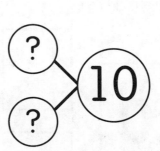

▪ **Model It**   **Find different ways to make 10.** ••••••••••••••••••

$1 +$ _____ $= 10$ _____ $+ 1 = 10$

$2 +$ _____ $= 10$ _____ $+ 2 = 10$

$3 +$ _____ $= 10$ _____ $+ 3 = 10$

$4 +$ _____ $= 10$ _____ $+ 4 = 10$

$5 +$ _____ $= 10$

Number Partners for 10

10 beads. 6 are red. The rest are yellow.
How many are yellow? How do you know?

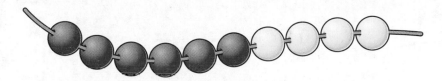

Model It Find 6 + ____ = 10.

Start with 6.
Add counters to make 10.
How many did you add?

 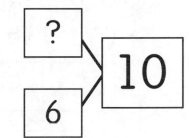

6 + ____ = 10

Talk About It **Who is right? How do you know?**

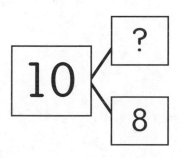

	Buzz writes:	Boom writes:
	10 + 8 = 2	8 + 2 = 10
	2 + 10 = 12	2 + 8 = 10
	8 = 10 − 2	8 = 10 − 2
	6 = 8 − 2	2 = 10 − 8

Number Partners for 10

Write two number sentences.

10 = _5_ + _5_

10 − _5_ = _5_

---

1 Complete the number bond.
Write two addition sentences.

```
[   ] [ 9 ]
     |
   [ 10 ]
```

10 = ___ + ___

___ + ___ = 10

---

2 Complete the number bond.
Write two subtraction sentences.

```
[   ] [ 9 ]
     |
   [ 10 ]
```

10 − 9 = ___

9 = 10 − ___

Number Partners for 10

3 Complete the number bond.
Write two subtraction sentences.

10 − ___ = ___

10 − ___ = ___

4 Complete the number bond.
Write two addition sentences.

10 = ___ + ___

___ + ___ = 10

5 Complete the number bond.
Write four number sentences.

___ + ___ = 10   10 − ___ = ___

10 = ___ + ___   ___ = 10 − ___

G Explore It

Yesterday there were 6 girls and 2 boys on the swings.
Today there are 4 boys and 4 girls on the swings.
How many children played on the swings each day?

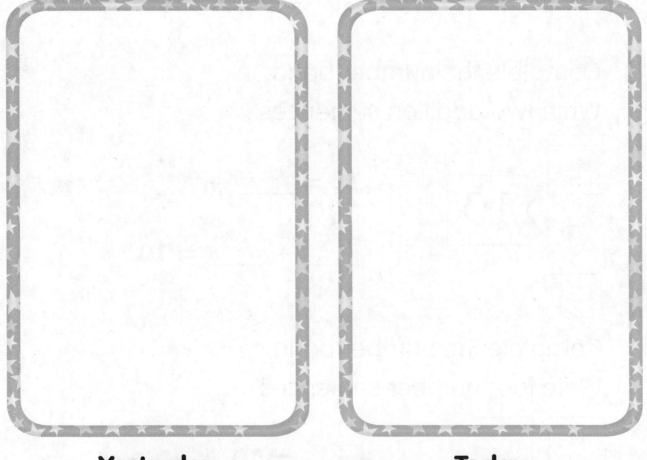

Yesterday   **Today**

____ + ____ = ____   ____ + ____ = ____

 **Try It**

Tom has 3 red beads and 4 yellow beads.
Dee has 2 blue beads and 5 green beads.
Do Tom and Dee each have the same number
of beads?

Tom's beads:

_____ + _____ = _____

Dee's beads:

_____ + _____ = _____

Explore Together
Understand the Equal Sign

What does = mean?

= is the **equal sign**.

= means **is the same as**.

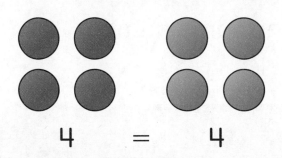

4 = 4

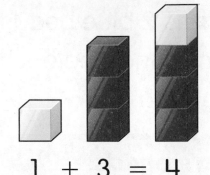

1 + 3 = 4

Think The total can go to the left or right of = .

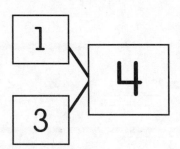

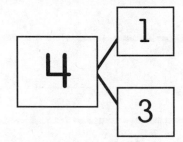

1 + 3 = ___   ___ = 1 + 3

Talk About It

4 + 2 = 5   5 = 2 + 3

Are both number sentences true?

How do you know?

Understand the Equal Sign

✋ **Find partners with equal totals.**

Look at the → Use cubes. → Complete the
numbers. Make partners. number sentences.

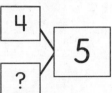
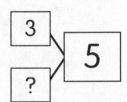

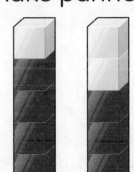

5 = 5

$4 + \underline{1} = 5$

$5 = 3 + \underline{2}$

$4 + \underline{1} = 3 + \underline{2}$

1 **Find partners with equal totals.**

2
6
?

6
?
3

$2 + \underline{} = 6$ $6 = \underline{} + 3$

$\underline{} + \underline{} = \underline{} + \underline{}$

💬 **Talk About It** •

Mia joins 2 cubes and 6 cubes.

Dan joins 4 cubes and 3 cubes.

Do they have the same number of cubes? How do you know?

Understand the Equal Sign

2 Draw Is $3 + 5 = 5 + 3$ a true number sentence? Draw to explain why or why not.

3 Evaluate Circle the true number sentences.

$$4 = 6 \qquad\qquad 7 = 4 + 3$$

$$1 + 3 = 2 + 2 \qquad\qquad 4 + 2 = 1 + 6$$

$$2 + 7 = 5 + 3 \qquad\qquad 8 + 2 = 4 + 6$$

4 Create Make true number sentences.

$$\underline{\hspace{1cm}} + \underline{\hspace{1cm}} = 3 + 7 \qquad\qquad 4 + 5 = \underline{\hspace{1cm}} + \underline{\hspace{1cm}}$$

Understand the Equal Sign

5 **Think about the equal sign.**

A: Write the number of shapes below each group.

Write = in the box if it is a true number sentence.

Write X in the box if it is not a true number sentence.

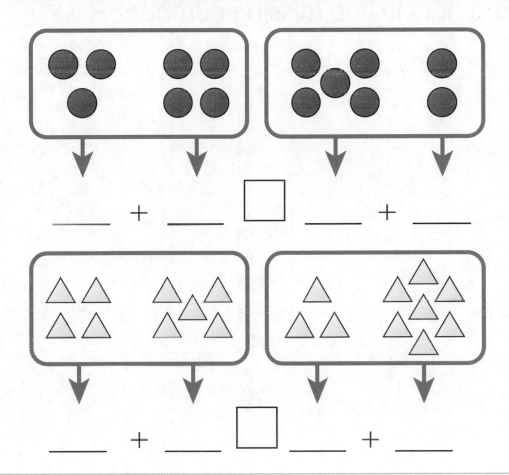

_____ + _____ ☐ _____ + _____

_____ + _____ ☐ _____ + _____

B: Use the number sentence that is not true.

Write a true number sentence. Show your work.

_____ + _____ ☐ _____ + _____

Independent Practice **Lesson 10**   **65**

 **Explore It**

Listen to the clues.

Use counters to find missing numbers.

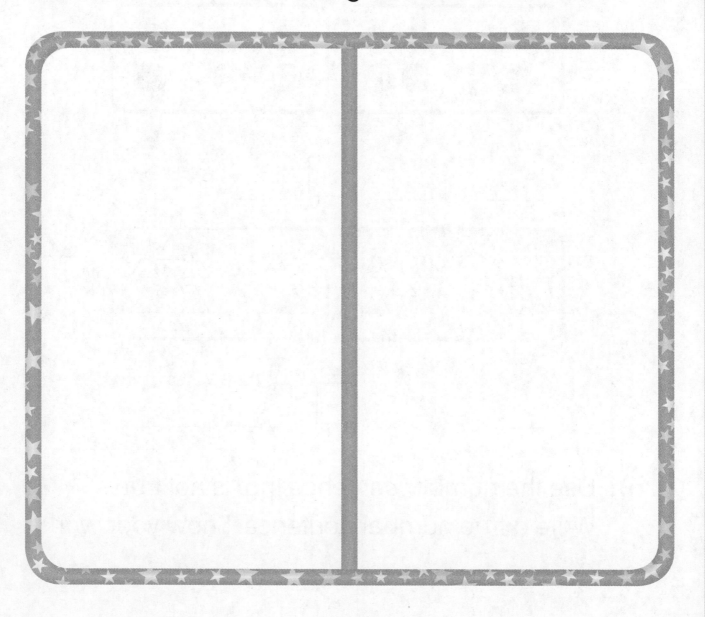

>> **Try It**

I have 8 marbles.

5 marbles are red, the rest are blue.

How many are blue?

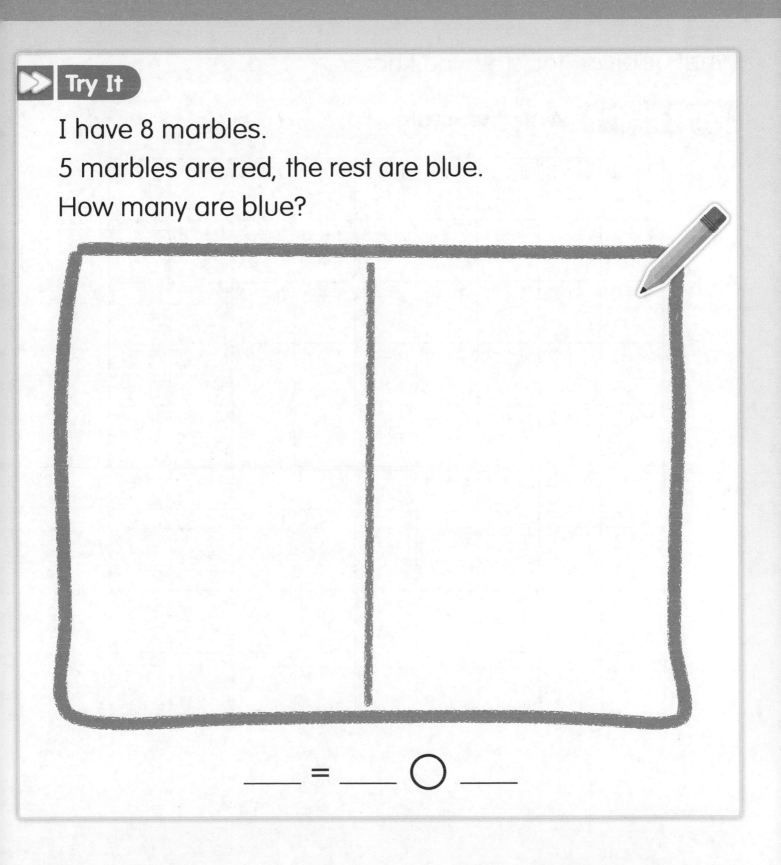

_____ = _____ ◯ _____

Facts I Know

What addition facts do you know?

 **Model It** Write the totals.

1 + 1	1 + 2	1 + 3	1 + 4	1 + 5	1 + 6	1 + 7	1 + 8	1 + 9
2 + 1	2 + 2	2 + 3	2 + 4	2 + 5	2 + 6	2 + 7	2 + 8	
3 + 1	3 + 2	3 + 3	3 + 4	3 + 5	3 + 6	3 + 7		
4 + 1	4 + 2	4 + 3	4 + 4	4 + 5	4 + 6			
5 + 1	5 + 2	5 + 3	5 + 4	5 + 5				
6 + 1	6 + 2	6 + 3	6 + 4					
7 + 1	7 + 2	7 + 3						
8 + 1	8 + 2							
9 + 1								

Facts I Know

What is the same about the facts in any row? What is different?

Model It Look at the facts in the colored boxes.

1 + 1 2	1 + 2 3	1 + 3 4	1 + 4 5	1 + 5 6	1 + 6 7	1 + 7 8	1 + 8 9	1 + 9 10
2 + 1 3	2 + 2 4	2 + 3 5	2 + 4 6	2 + 5 7	2 + 6 8	2 + 7 9	2 + 8 10	
3 + 1 4	3 + 2 5	3 + 3 6	3 + 4 7	3 + 5 8	3 + 6 9	3 + 7 10		
4 + 1 5	4 + 2 6	4 + 3 7	4 + 4 8	4 + 5 9	4 + 6 10			
5 + 1 6	5 + 2 7	5 + 3 8	5 + 4 9	5 + 5 10				
6 + 1 7	6 + 2 8	6 + 3 9	6 + 4 10					
7 + 1 8	7 + 2 9	7 + 3 10						
8 + 1 9	8 + 2 10							
9 + 1 10								

Talk About It

How can the table help you learn addition facts?

Practice Together
Facts I Know

Fill in the blanks.

1

4 + ____ 7	____ + 4 8	4 + 5 ____	____ + ____ 10
____ + 3 8	5 + ____ 9	____ + ____ 10	

2

____ + 1 8	7 + ____ 9	____ + ____ 10
8 + ____ 9	____ + 2 10	

3

2 + ____ 6	____ + 5 7	2 + 6 ____	____ + 7 ____	2 + ____ 10
____ + 4 7	3 + ____ 8	____ + ____ 9	3 + ____ ____	

Practice by Myself
Facts I Know

4 Fill in the table.

Partners of 7	Partners of 8	Partners of 9	Partners of 10
0 + 7 = ___	0 + 8 = ___		
1 + ___ = 7			
___ + 5 = 7			
3 + ___ = 7			
4 + ___ = 7			
___ + 2 = 7			
6 + ___ = 7			
___ + 0 = 7			

Unit 2 Review

Solve the problems.

1 Al has 5 toy trucks. He has 5 toy cars. How many toy trucks and cars does Al have?

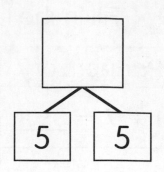

$5 + 5 =$ _____

2 There are 3 birds. More birds join them. Now there are 7 birds. How many birds join?

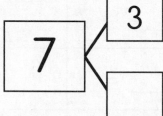

$3 +$ _____ $= 7$

3 Make a true number sentence.

_____ $+$ _____ $= 2 + 7$

4 $10 - 8 =$ _____

5 _____ $= 5 + 2$

6 Make a true number sentence.

$5 +$ _____ $= 3 + 5$

7 4 books and 2 books. How many books in all?

4 + 2 = _____   _____ = 2 + 4

Is 4 + 2 = 2 + 4 a true number sentence? _____
Draw to explain why or why not.

---

8 10 beads in all.

3 are red. The rest are yellow.
How many are yellow?

Complete the number bond.
Write four number sentences
for this problem.

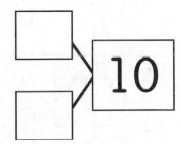

_____ + _____ = 10   10 − _____ = _____

10 = _____ + _____   _____ = 10 − _____

Put It Together

9 **Use the partners of 8 or 9.**

Write all the partners of 8 or 9 in the number bonds. Then write a true number sentence. Use two different partners. Explain how you know your number sentence is true.

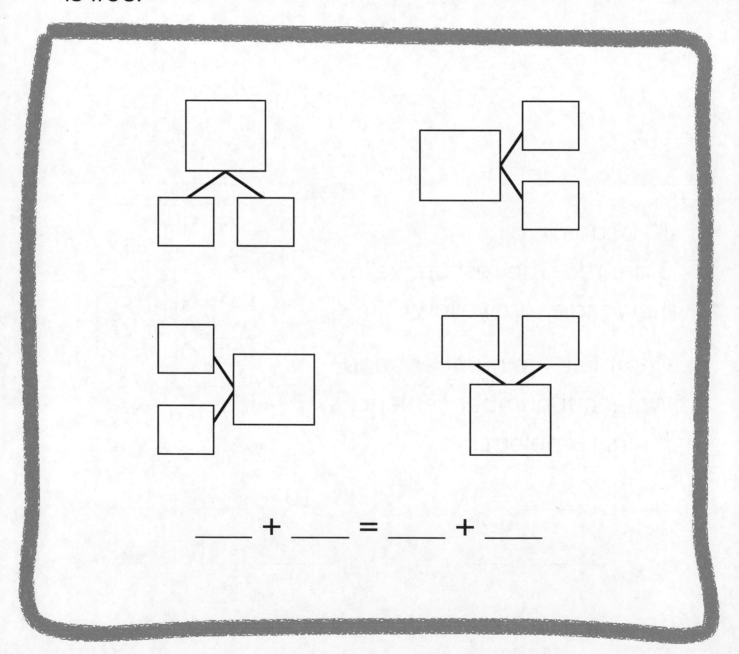

_____ + _____ = _____ + _____

©Curriculum Associates, LLC Copying is not permitted.

Danna wants to give some apples to her aunt. She wants to keep some apples for herself. What math questions could Danna ask about the apples?

In this unit, you will learn ways to add and subtract within 20. Then you will be able to solve problems like Danna's.

✓ Self Check

Check off the skills you know now. Then see how many more you can check off after each lesson!

I can:	Before this unit	After this unit
name and write teen numbers.	☐	☐
make totals greater than 10.	☐	☐
make a ten to add.	☐	☐
add three numbers.	☐	☐
make a ten to subtract.	☐	☐
solve addition and subtraction word problems.	☐	☐

Explore It

Show 13.

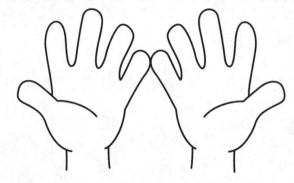 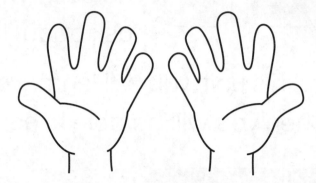

Show 16.

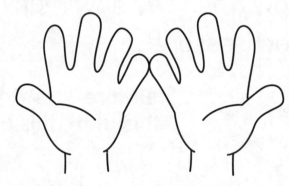 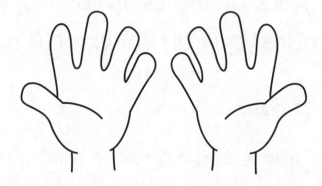

Show 19.

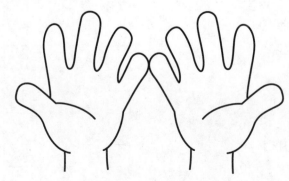 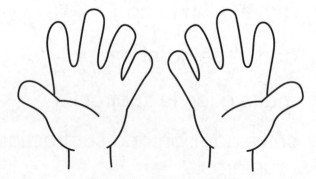

>> **Try It**

Draw or trace to show 14 fingers.
Show how you know there are 14.

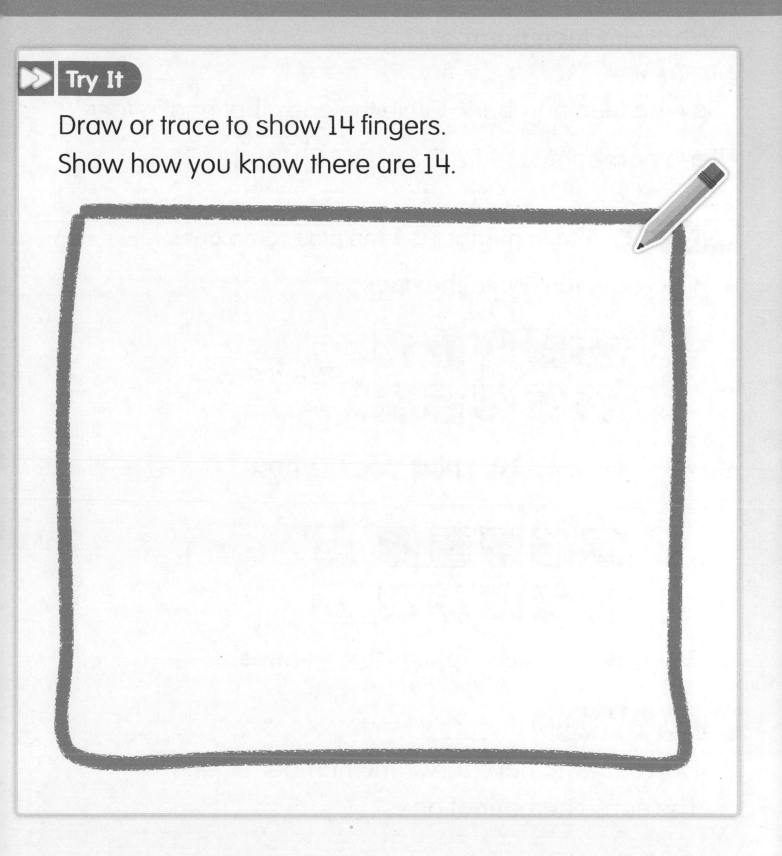

Understand Teen Numbers

What are teen numbers?

Say the teen numbers. Circle the ones that end in *teen*.

Teen numbers: 11, 12, 13, 14, 15, 16, 17, 18, 19

 **Think** A teen number is 1 ten plus some ones. · · · · · · · · · · · ·

Circle the ten. Write the ones.

11 **is** **10** **plus** ____ **one**

12 **is** **10** **plus** ____ **ones**

 **Talk About It** ·

Do 10 and 11 have the same number of tens?

The same number of ones?

Understand Teen Numbers

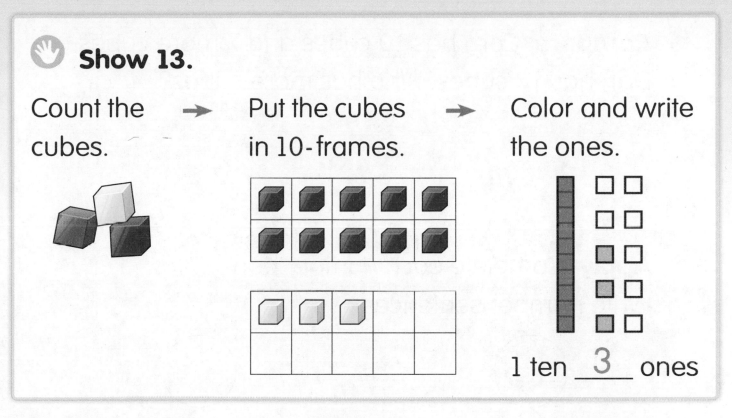

✋ **Show 13.**

Count the cubes. → Put the cubes in 10-frames. → Color and write the ones.

1 ten __3__ ones

---

1 **Show 14.**

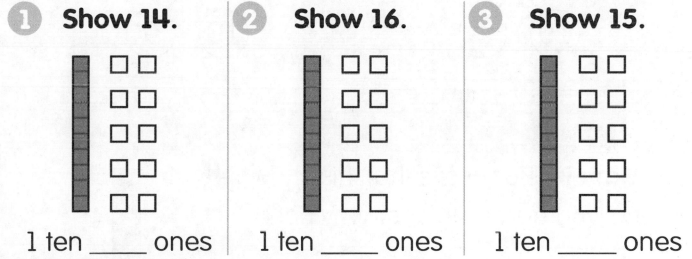

1 ten ____ ones

2 **Show 16.**

1 ten ____ ones

3 **Show 15.**

1 ten ____ ones

💬 **Talk About It** •

What is the same about the teen numbers?
What is different?

Connect It
Understand Teen Numbers

④ Compare Cora has 10 cubes and 7 more cubes. Dan has 18 cubes. Who has more cubes?

⑤ Apply Complete each number bond. Write number sentences.

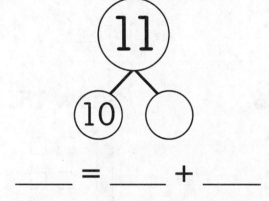
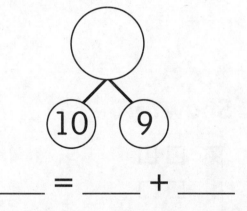

___ = ___ + ___   ___ = ___ + ___

⑥ Explain Buzz says that this shows 4. Do you agree? Why or why not?

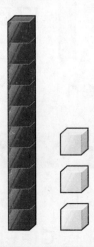

©Curriculum Associates, LLC   Copying is not permitted.

Understand Teen Numbers

7 **Think about teen numbers.**

A: Draw more stickers.

Make two different teen numbers.

B: Make number bonds for your teen numbers.

Then write your teen numbers.

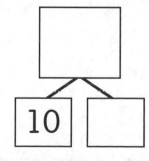

|10| |

____ is the same as

____ ten ____ ones

|10| |

____ is the same as

____ ten ____ ones

G **Explore It**

Find ways to make 11.

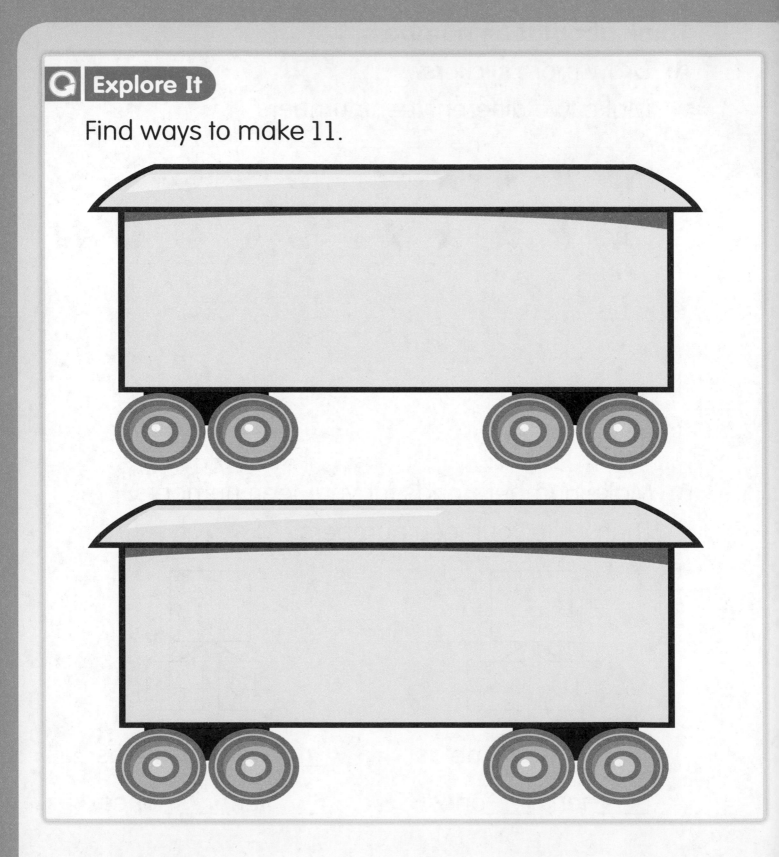

 **Try It**

Show ways to make 11.

$11 = 10 + \underline{}$

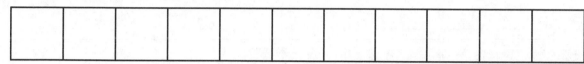

$11 = 9 + \underline{}$

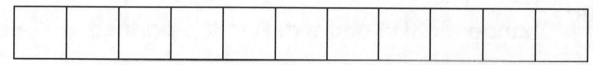

$11 = 8 + \underline{}$

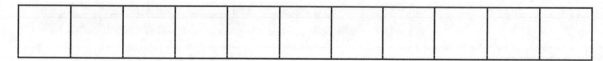

$11 = 7 + \underline{}$

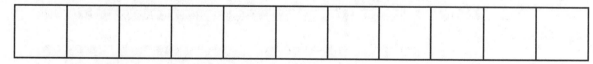

$11 = 6 + \underline{}$

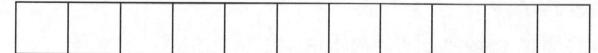

Understand Sums Greater than 10

How do you find partners of teen numbers?

You know that 12 is 10 + 2.

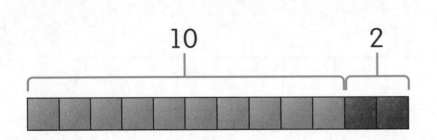

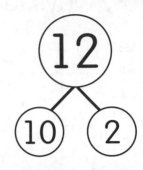

Think Change the first addend. Find the partner.

12 = 10 + 2

12 = 9 + 3

12 = 8 + ____

12 = 7 + ____

12 = 6 + ____

Talk About It

Change the order of the addends.
What happens when you add?

©Curriculum Associates, LLC   Copying is not permitted.

Understand Sums Greater than 10

 10 + ? = 13

Use cubes. → Find the partner. → Complete the number bond and number sentence.

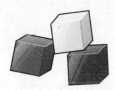

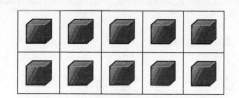

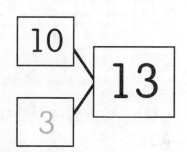

$$10 + \underline{\quad 3 \quad} = 13$$

---

① 9 + ? = 13

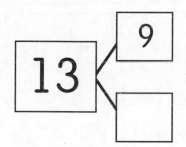

$$9 + \underline{\quad\quad} = 13$$

② 8 + ? = 13

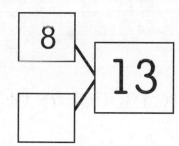

$$8 + \underline{\quad\quad} = 13$$

③ 7 + ? = 13

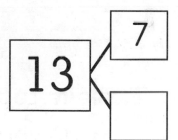

$$7 + \underline{\quad\quad} = 13$$

 Talk About It •

How did you find the partners of 13?

Understand Sums Greater than 10

4 **Interpret** Complete the number bond and number sentences.

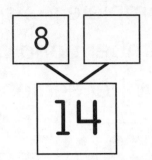

$14 = 8 +$ _____

$14 =$ _____ $+ 8$

5 **Illustrate** Use two colors. Color the circles. Then complete the number sentences.

$9 +$ _____ $= 14$

_____ $+ 9 = 14$

6 **Explain** Look at the model. Is Buzz correct? How do you know?

Buzz writes:

$8 + 6 = 15$

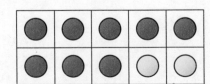 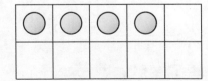

Understand Sums Greater than 10

7 **Think about different ways to make totals greater than 10.**

A: Draw to show partners of 15.

Complete the number bonds.

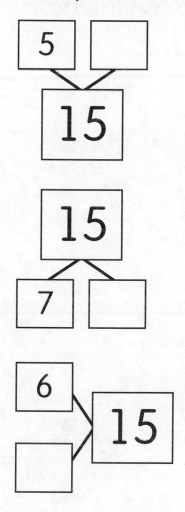

B: Show all of the partners of 16.

Make a Ten to Add

7 children get on the bus. 5 more children get on the bus. How many children are on the bus?

 **Try It**

9 children get on the bus. 5 more children get on the bus. How many children are on the bus?

9 and 5 is the same as 10 and _____ more.

_____ children are on the bus.

Explore Together
Make a Ten to Add

8 children are on the bus. 5 more get on the bus.
How many are on the bus now?

$$8 + 5 = ?$$

▦ Model It **Find 8 + 5.** •

Start with 8. Take counters from 5 to **make a ten**.

8   **+**   **5**   **= ____**

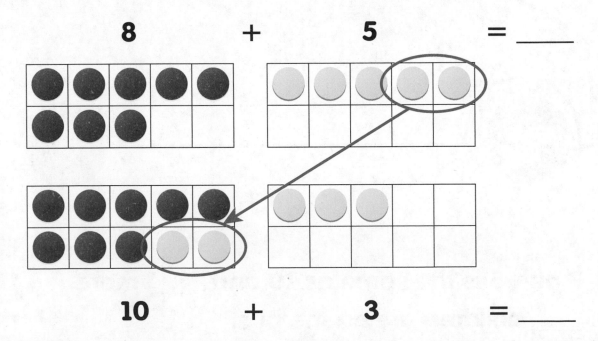

10   **+**   **3**   **= ____**

90 **Lesson 14** Modeled Instruction

Make a Ten to Add

7 blocks are small. 5 blocks are big.

How many blocks are there in all?

How do you know?

7 + 5 = ?

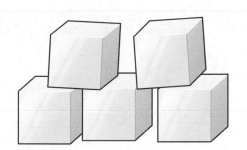

Model It Find 7 + 5.

Start with 7.

Add 3 to make 10.

Then add 2 more.

$7 + 3 = 10$ $10 + 2 = 12$

7 + 5 = _____

Talk About It Do you agree? Why or why not?

Boom says that $9 + 5 = 15$.

 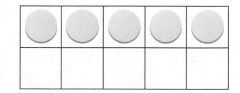

Practice Together
Make a Ten to Add

8 + 6 = ?

8 + 2 = <u>10</u>

10 + 4 = <u>14</u>

So, 8 + 6 = <u>14</u>

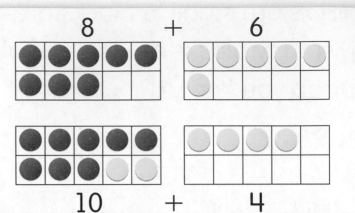

8   +   6

10   +   4

---

1   8 + 7 = ?

    8 + ____ = 10

    10 + ____ = ____

    8 + 7 = ____

---

2   7 + 7 = ?

| 6 | 7 | 8 | 9 | 10 | 11 | 12 | 13 | 14 | 15 |

    7 + ____ = 10

    10 + ____ = ____

    7 + 7 = ____

Make a Ten to Add

3 7 + 6 = ?

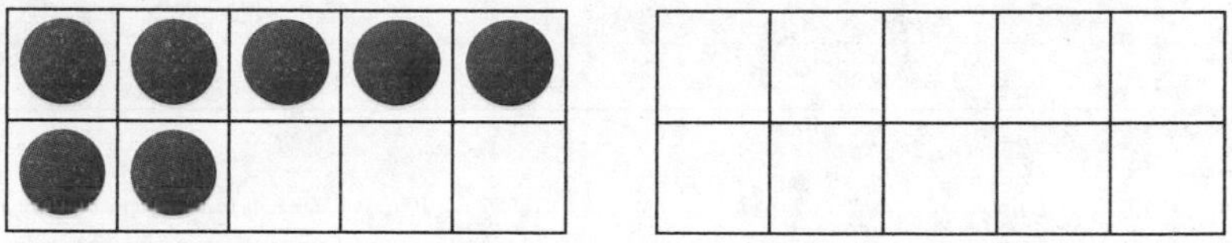

7 + ___ = ___

10 + ___ = ___

7 + 6 = ___

4 9 + 4 = ?

| 6 | 7 | 8 | ⑨ | 10 | 11 | 12 | 13 | 14 | 15 |

9 + 4 = ___

5 8 + 9 = ?

8 + 9 = ___

Add Three Numbers

G **Explore It**

Joe picks up 7 pencils. Carla picks up 3 pencils. Pete picks up 4 pencils. How many pencils do the children pick up?

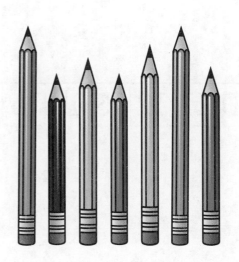 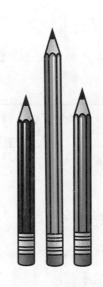 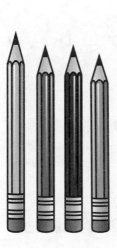

____ + ____ + ____ = ?

____

____ + ____ = ____

____ + ____ + ____ = ?

____

____ + ____ = ____

The children pick up _____ pencils.

Try It

Ana has 6 red blocks, 4 blue blocks, and 2 green blocks. How many blocks does she have in all?

6 + 4 + 2 = ?

_____

___ + ___ = ___

6 + 2 + 4 = ?

_____

___ + ___ = ___

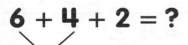 **Ana has _____ blocks in all.**

Explore Together
Add Three Numbers

Pat collects 8 cans of food.

Max collects 2 cans. May collects 4 cans.

How many cans do they collect in all?

Model It Find 8 + 2 + 4. •

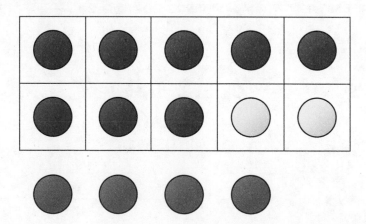

$$8 + 2 + 4$$
$$10 + 4 = \underline{\qquad}$$

Add Three Numbers

Adam plants 6 flowers. Kate plants 4 flowers.
Yuri plants 8 flowers. How many flowers?
How do you know?

Model It Find 6 + 4 + 8.

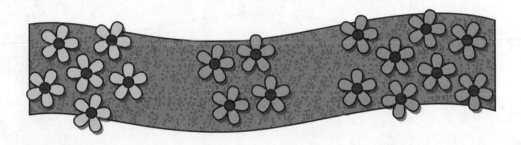

6 + 4 = _____

10 + _____ = _____

Talk About It Do you agree? Why or why not?

Boom writes 6 + 4 + 8.

Buzz writes 4 + 6 + 8.

Buzz says both are correct.

Practice Together
Add Three Numbers

Jon has 7 apples. Tom has 3 apples.
Bo has 5 apples. How many apples do
they have?

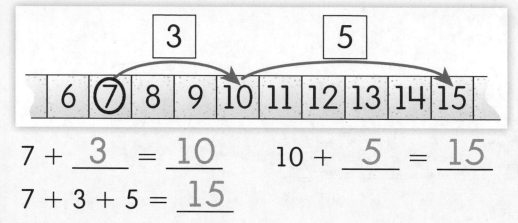

$$7 + \underline{\ 3\ } = \underline{\ 10\ } \qquad 10 + \underline{\ 5\ } = \underline{\ 15\ }$$

$$7 + 3 + 5 = \underline{\ 15\ }$$

1 Ann has 9 red balls and 1 green ball.
She has 2 blue balls. How many balls does she have?

$$\underline{\quad} + \underline{\quad} = \mathbf{10}$$

$$\mathbf{10} + \underline{\quad} = \underline{\quad}$$

2 Deb has 8 round stickers.
She has 4 square stickers
and 6 triangle stickers.
How many stickers does Deb have?

$$\mathbf{8 + 4 + 6}$$

$$\underline{\quad} + \underline{\quad} = \underline{\quad}$$

Add Three Numbers

3 Bob has 5 books. Jill gives him 3 more books. Then he gets 5 more books. How many books does Bob have now?

| 5 | 6 | 7 | 8 | 9 | 10 | 11 | 12 | 13 | 14 |

10

$5 + 3 + 5 = \underline{\hspace{1cm}}$

4 8 children are on the bus. 2 more children get on. 9 children get on next. How many children are on the bus now?

10

$8 + 2 + 9 = \underline{\hspace{1cm}}$

5 There are 6 marbles in a jar. Len puts 3 marbles in. Pam puts 7 marbles in. How many marbles are in the jar now?

$6 + 3 + 7 = \underline{\hspace{1cm}}$

G | **Explore It**

Maria has 16 markers. 9 fall out of her bag.
How many markers are left?

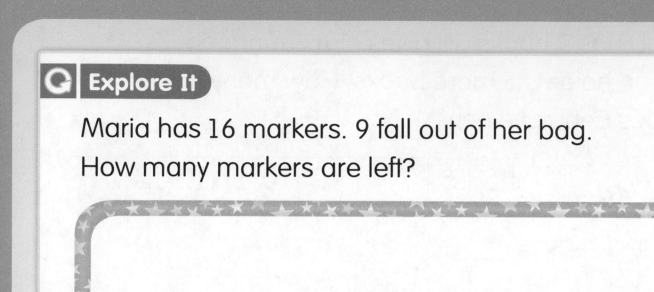

_____ − _____ = _____

 Try It

Rina has 13 apples. She gives away 6 apples.
How many apples does she have left?

_____ – _____ = _____

Make a Ten to Subtract

Ava has 15 beads. She gives away 7 beads.
How many beads are left?

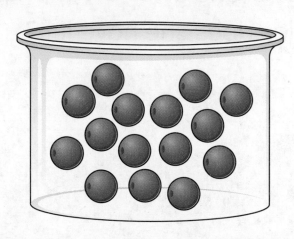

Model It   **Find 15 − 7.** ••••••••••••••••••••••••••••••••••••••

$15 - 7 = ?$ is the same as $7 + ? = 15$

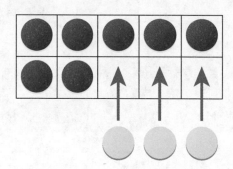   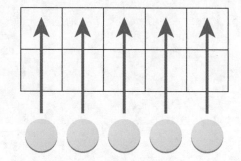

Start with 7.

How many more to 10? __3__

How many more to 15? ____

So, $15 - 7 = $ ____

Learn Together
Make a Ten to Subtract

Coach has 14 hats. He gives out 6 hats.
How many hats are left?

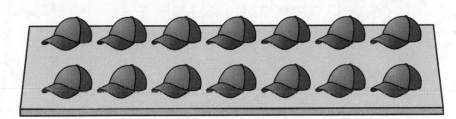

Model It Find 14 − 6. Think: 6 = 2 + 4. ·····················

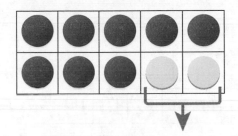   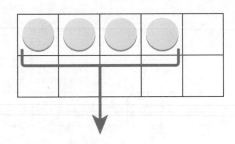

$$14 - 4 = \underline{\hphantom{000}}$$

$$10 - 2 = \underline{\hphantom{000}}$$

$$14 - 6 = \underline{\hphantom{000}}$$

Take away 2.   Take away 4.

Talk About It What is wrong? ·····················

Buzz finds 13 − 5.

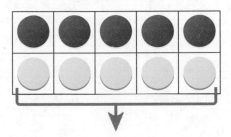   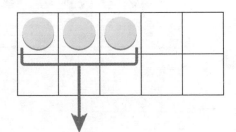

Take away 5.   Take away 3.

Practice Together
Make a Ten to Subtract

$16 - 7 = ?$

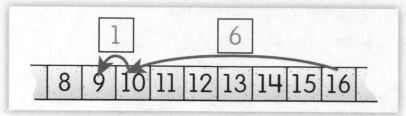

$16 - \underline{6} = 10$

$10 - \underline{1} = \underline{9}$

So, $16 - 7 = \underline{9}$

1 $14 - 9 = ?$

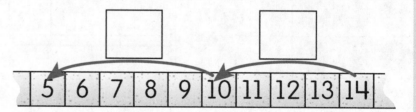

$14 - \underline{} = 10$

$10 - \underline{} = \underline{}$

$14 - 9 = \underline{}$

2 $17 - 8 = ?$

$17 - \underline{} = 10$

$10 - \underline{} = \underline{}$

$17 - 8 = \underline{}$

Make a Ten to Subtract

3 13 − 7 = ?

13 − 7 = _____

4 15 − 8 = ?

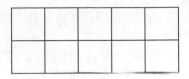

15 − 8 = _____

5 14 − 5 = ?

14 − 5 = _____

Solve the problems.

1 8 blocks are big. 7 blocks are small.
How many in all?

8 + ____ = ____

10 + ____ = ____

8 + 7 = ____

---

2 Max has 14 stickers. He gives away 5 stickers.
How many stickers are left?

| 6 | 7 | 8 | 9 | 10 | 11 | 12 | 13 | 14 | 15 |

14 − ____ = 10

10 − ____ = ____

14 − 5 = ____

---

3 4 green balls. 7 red balls. 3 blue balls.
How many in all?

4 + 7 + 3 = ____

4 ____ = 13 − 6

---

5 16 is the same as

____ ten and ____ ones

6 17 = 10 + ____

17 = ____ + 8

7 6 children are on the bus.
5 more children get on.
4 children get on next.
How many children are
on the bus now?

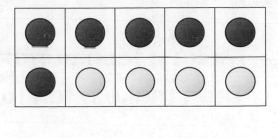

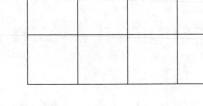

$$\overset{10}{\underset{6 + 5 + 4}{\diagup\diagdown}} = \underline{\quad}$$

There are _____ children on the bus now.

---

8 Cam has 11 apples.
9 are red. The rest are green.
Complete the number bonds.
Then write two addition sentences.

_____ + 1 = 11

9 + _____ = 11

Cam has _____ green apples.

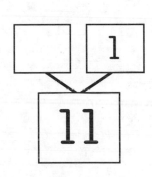

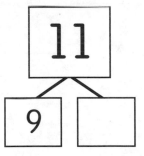

9 **Make a teen number.**

Then make a ten to subtract.

Draw more stickers to make 11, 12, 13, 14, or 15.

Then subtract 7 from your number.

____ − ____ = 10

10 − ____ = ____

So, ____ − 7 = ____

 The cherries and grapes are in bags of 10. Ben gives Emma some of the bags. What math questions could Ben ask about the bags of fruit?

In this unit, you will learn about tens and how to add and subtract tens. Then you will be able to solve problems like Ben's.

✓ Self Check

Check off the skills you know now. Then see how many more you can check off after each lesson!

I can:	Before this unit	After this unit
show numbers as tens.	☐	☐
count on a 120 chart.	☐	☐
find 10 more and 10 less than a number.	☐	☐
subtract 10 in my head.	☐	☐
add tens.	☐	☐
subtract tens.	☐	☐

G Explore It

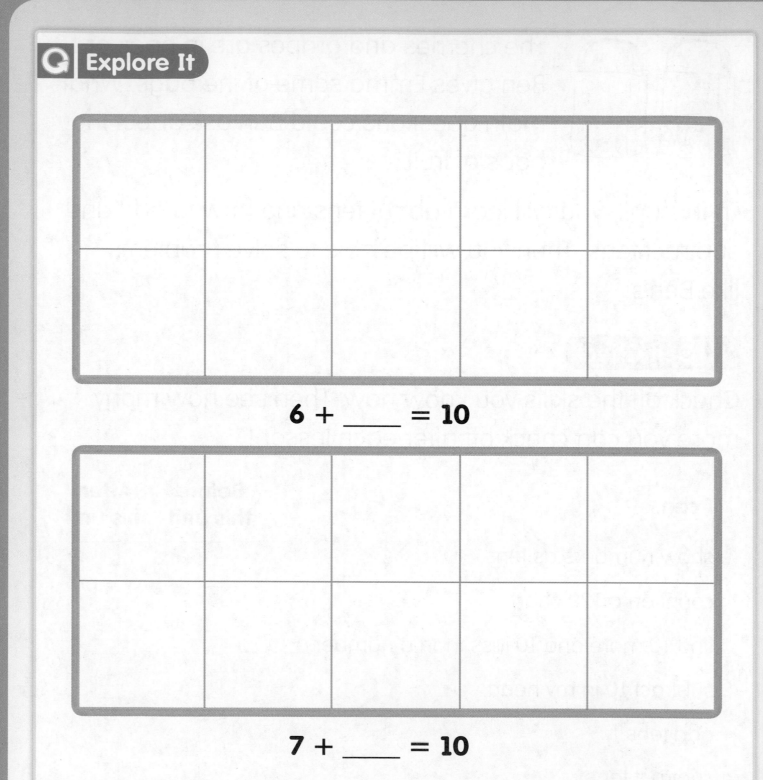

6 + _____ = 10

7 + _____ = 10

▶▶ Try It

_____ **tens**   _____ **ones**

Explore Together
Understand Tens

What is a ten?

Ten is
10 ones.

Ten is the name for
a group of 10 ones.

 **Think** **What is 2 tens?** •

2 **tens** is

___ groups of 10.

2 tens is

___ ones.

 Talk About It •

Look at the picture of 10 ones and the picture of 1 ten.
How are they the same?

Explore Together
Understand Tens

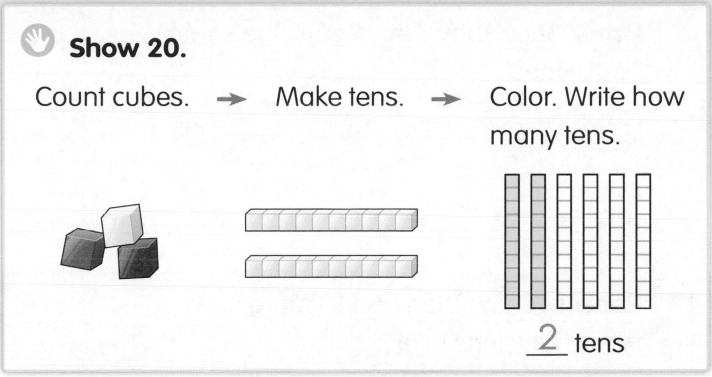

✋ **Show 20.**

Count cubes. → Make tens. → Color. Write how many tens.

_2_ tens

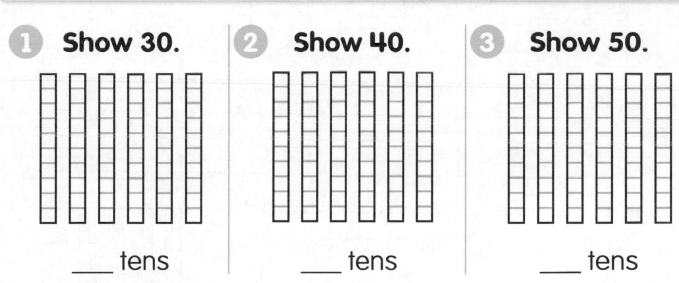

1 **Show 30.**

___ tens

2 **Show 40.**

___ tens

3 **Show 50.**

___ tens

💬 **Talk About It** •

Ana counts 3 tens. Micah counts 20 ones. Which is more?

Understand Tens

4 **Draw** Show why 1 ten means the same as 10 ones.

5 **Reason** Draw 1 ten and 10 more ones. How many tens in all?

6 **Explain** David says this shows 14. Do you agree? Why or why not?

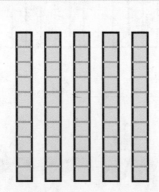

Understand Tens

7 **Think about making tens.**

   A: Circle groups of 10.
      Write how many.

★★★★★★★★★★★★
★★★★★★★★★★★
★★★★★★★★★★

How many groups? ____

How many stars?   ____

How many groups? ____

How many flowers? ____

How many groups? ____

How many stars?   ____

   B: Draw 21 beach balls.
      Show how you know you have 21.

The 120 Chart

Q | **Explore It**

How can you count on a 120 chart?

1	2	3	4	5	6	7	8	9	10
11	12	13	14	15	16	17	18	19	20
21	22	23	24	25	26	27	28	29	30
31	32	33	34	35	36	37	38	39	40
41	42	43	44	45	46	47	48	49	50
51	52	53	54	55	56	57	58	59	60
61	62	63	64	65	66	67	68	69	70
71	72	73	74	75	76	77	78	79	80
81	82	83	84	85	86	87	88	89	90
91	92	93	94	95	96	97	98	99	100
101	102	103	104	105	106	107	108	109	110
111	112	113	114	115	116	117	118	119	120

 **Try It**

Write the missing numbers.

31	32	33		35	36	37	38	39	40
41	42	43	44	45	46	47	48	49	
51	52	53	54	55		57	58	59	60

81	82	83	84	85	86		88	89	90
91		93	94	95	96	97	98	99	
101	102	103	104			107	108	109	110

The 120 Chart

How does the 120 chart show numbers?

Model It **Find numbers.** •

Use blue. Color the numbers that have 2 ones.

Use red. Circle the numbers that have 3 tens.

1	2	3	4	5	6	7	8	9	10
11	12	13	14	15	16	17	18	19	20
21	22	23	24	25	26	27	28	29	30
31	32	33	34	35	36	37	38	39	40
41	42	43	44	45	46	47	48	49	50
51	52	53	54	55	56	57	58	59	60
61	62	63	64	65	66	67	68	69	70
71	72	73	74	75	76	77	78	79	80
81	82	83	84	85	86	87	88	89	90
91	92	93	94	95	96	97	98	99	100
101	102	103	104	105	106	107	108	109	110
111	112	113	114	115	116	117	118	119	120

The 120 Chart

How can you count on the 120 chart?

Model It **Count up.** ·······································

Count up 1 from 5. Then count up 1 from 18.

5 and 1 more is ____.

18 and 1 more is ____.

1	2	3	4	⑤	**6**	7	8	9	10
11	12	13	14	15	16	17	⑱	**19**	20

Count up 2 from 62. Then count up 2 from 75.

62 and 2 more is ____.

75 and 2 more is ____.

61	㊷	63	**64**	65	66	67	68	69	70
71	72	73	74	㊵	76	**77**	78	79	80

Count up 5 from 85. Then count up 5 from 90.

85 and 5 more is ____.

90 and 5 more is ____.

81	82	83	84	㊧	86	87	88	89	⑨⓪
91	92	93	94	**95**	96	97	98	99	100

Talk About It **Who is right? How do you know?** ···········

Boom says 70 and 5 more is 74.

Buzz says 70 and 5 more is 75.

Practice Together
The 120 Chart

Fill in the blanks. Use the chart.

31	32	33	34	35	36	37	38	39	40
41	42	43	44	45	46	47	48	49	50
51	52	53	54	55	56	57	58	59	60

1 **Start at 40.**   **Start at 55.**

1 more than 40 is ____.   1 more than 55 is ____.

2 more than 40 is ____.   2 more than 55 is ____.

5 more than 40 is ____.   5 more than 55 is ____.

2 **Count by 1:**   33, ____, 35, ____, 37, ____

Count by 2:   42, ____, ____, ____, 50

Count by 5:   40, 45, ____, ____, ____

The 120 Chart

Fill in the blanks. Use the chart.

91	92	93	94	95	96	97	98	99	100
101	102	103	104	105	106	107	108	109	110
111	112	113	114	115	116	117	118	119	120

3 | **Start at 100.** | **Start at 115.**

1 more than 100 is ____. | 1 more than 115 is ____.

2 more than 100 is ____. | 2 more than 115 is ____.

5 more than 100 is ____. | 5 more than 115 is ____.

4 **Count by 1:** 104, ____, 106, ____, 108, ____

Count by 2: 98, ____, ____, ____, 106

Count by 5: 95, 100, ____, ____, ____

G | **Explore It**

There are 27 monkeys living at the zoo.
There are 10 more birds than monkeys.
How many birds live at the zoo?

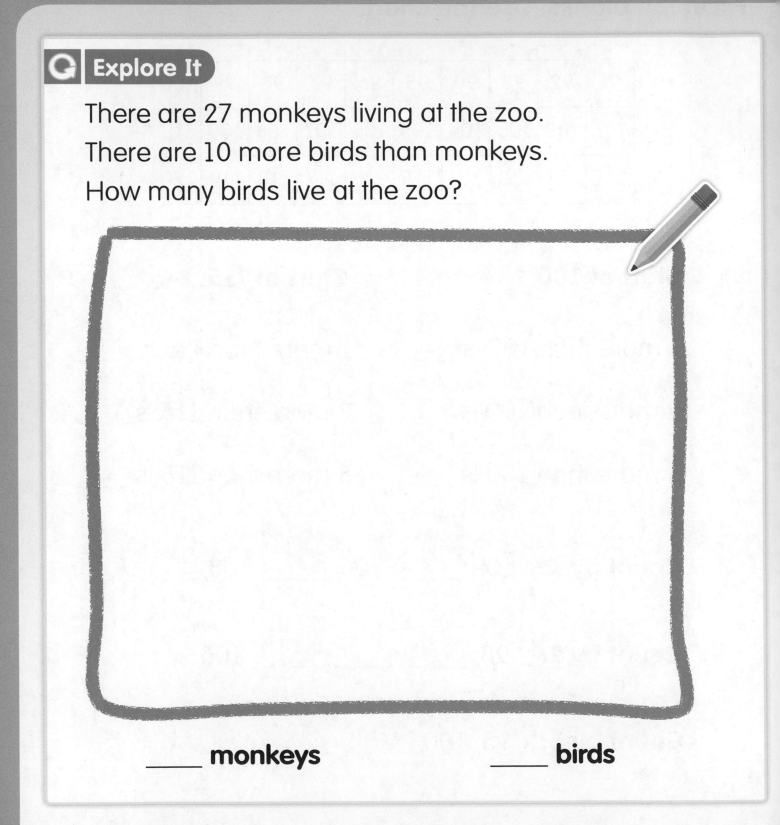

_____ **monkeys**   _____ **birds**

>> **Try It**

What is 10 more than 31?

10 more than 31 is _____ .

What is 10 less than 31?

10 less than 31 is _____ .

Explore Together
Understand 10 More and 10 Less

> ## What is 10 more and 10 less?

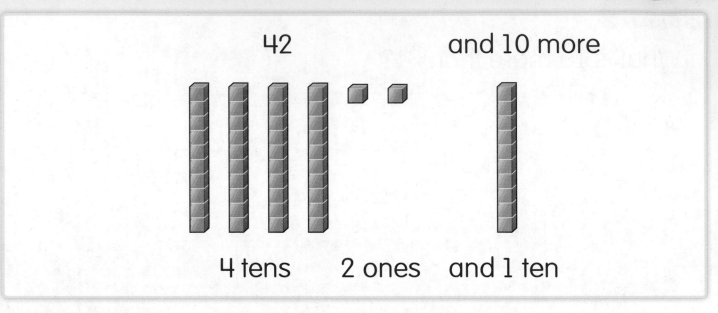

42   and 10 more

4 tens   2 ones   and 1 ten

Think **10 more means adding 1 ten.** ································

$$42 + 10 = 52$$

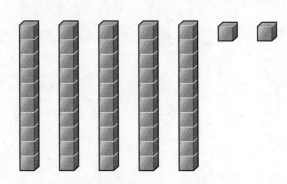

____ tens   ____ ones

 **Talk About It** ···

How do the digits change when you add 10 to 42?

Explore Together
Understand 10 More and 10 Less

 Find 10 less than 37.

Use a 120 chart. ➔ Color the ➔ __27__ is 10
Color 37.   number   less than 37.
                   above 37.

21	22	23	24	25	26	27	28	29	30
31	32	33	34	35	36	37	38	39	40
41	42	43	44	45	46	47	48	49	50

1 **Find 10 more than 62.**
Color both numbers.

____ is 10 more than 62.

2 **Find 10 less than 69.**
Color both numbers.

____ is 10 less than 69.

51	52	53	54	55	56	57	58	59	60
61	62	63	64	65	66	67	68	69	70
71	72	73	74	75	76	77	78	79	80

💬 Talk About It •

How does the 120 chart help you find 10 less
and 10 more? Why does this work?

Understand 10 More and 10 Less

③ Identify What is 10 more than 96?

81	82	83	84	85	86	87	88	89	90
91	92	93	94	95	96	97	98	99	100
101	102	103	104	105	106	107	108	109	110

10 more than 96 is _____.

④ Choose Fill in the blanks. Use the numbers in the box.

_____ is 10 more than 58.

_____ is 10 less than 58.

_____ is 10 more than 88.

_____ is 10 less than 88.

78

48

68

98

⑤ Explain Buzz says 10 less than 84 is 83.
Do you agree? Why or why not?

Understand 10 More and 10 Less

6 **Think about 10 more and 10 less.**

A: Use digit cards to make numbers.

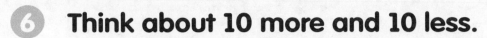

Write a number. Find 10 less and 10 more than your number.

☐ ☐   10 less than ____ is ____.

10 more than ____ is ____.

Write a different number. Find 10 less and 10 more than your number.

☐ ☐   10 less than ____ is ____.

10 more than ____ is ____.

B: Find 93 + 10. Tell how you know.

93 + 10 = ____

 **Explore It**

Buzz uses 30 foam shapes. He then uses 20 more.
How many shapes does Buzz use in all?

Buzz uses _____ shapes in all.

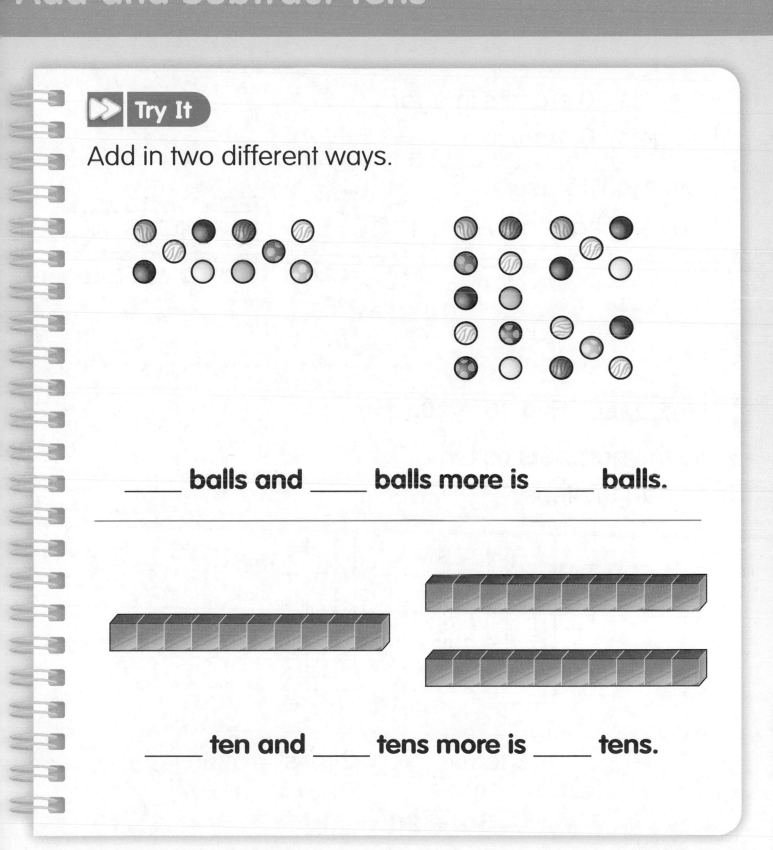

▶▶ **Try It**

Add in two different ways.

_____ **balls and** _____ **balls more is** _____ **balls.**

_____ **ten and** _____ **tens more is** _____ **tens.**

Add and Subtract Tens

Tess has 30 erasers in a jar.
She gets 20 more.

How many erasers
does she have now?

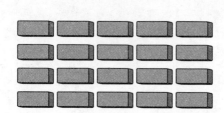

▦ Model It   Find 30 + 20. ●

Write the numbers as tens.
Then add the tens.

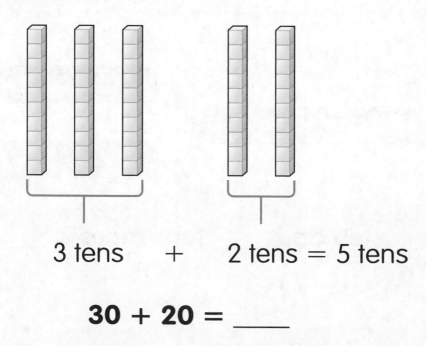

3 tens   +   2 tens = 5 tens

30 + 20 = ____

Add and Subtract Tens

Julie picks 70 berries.
Al picks 40 berries.

How many more
does Julie pick?

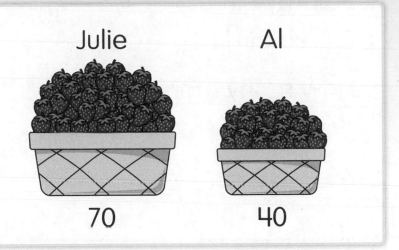

Julie   Al

70   40

Model It   **Find 70 − 40.**

Use addition to subtract.

Write as tens.

Then add the tens.

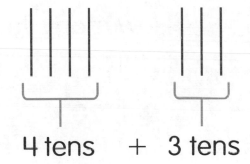

4 tens   +   3 tens

40 + ? = 70

4 tens + _____ tens = _____ tens

70 − 40 = _____

Talk About It   **Who is right? How do you know?**

Buzz says 60 − 20 = 40.

Boom says 6 tens − 2 tens = 4 tens.

Practice Together
Add and Subtract Tens

50 gray birds.
30 red birds.

How many more
gray birds?

50 − 30 = __20__

$30 + ? = 50$

| | | | |

3 tens   2 tens

---

1 10 blue flowers.
20 yellow flowers.

How many flowers
in all?

10 + 20 = ___   ___ **ten +** ___ **tens =** ___ **tens**

---

2 Find 90 − 40.

$4 + ? = 9$

4 tens + ____ **tens = 9 tens**

40 + ____ **= 90**   **90 − 40 =** ____

Practice by Myself
Add and Subtract Tens

3 60 paper clips.
50 are in a box.

How many are not
in the box?

$50 + ? = 60$

| | | | | |

60 − 50 = ____

4 30 footballs and 30 basketballs.

What is the total number of balls?

30 + 30 = ____

____ tens + ____ tens = ____ tens

5 Find 80 − 20.

$2 + ? = 8$

2 tens + ____ tens = 8 tens

20 + ____ = 80   **80 − 20 = ____**

Unit 4 Review

Solve the problems.

1 35 ducks and 2 more ducks.

2 more than 35 is _____.

23	24	25	26	27	28
33	34	35	36	37	38
43	44	45	46	47	48

---

2 52 paper clips. 10 are in a box.
How many are not in the box?

41	42	43	44	45	46	47	48	49	50
51	52	53	54	55	56	57	58	59	60
61	62	63	64	65	66	67	68	69	70

52 − 10 = _____

---

3 **86 + 10 = _____**   **4** **_____ = 80 − 10**

---

5 **Count by 1: 108, _____, 110, _____, _____, 113**

6 The number of birds is the same as 6 tens.

Draw 6 tens.

6 tens is _____ groups of 10.   6 tens is _____ ones.

There are _____ birds.

---

7 Jo has 24 markers.

24 is _____ tens and _____ ones.

Bo has 10 more than Jo.   Mo has 10 fewer than Jo.

_____ $= 24 + 10$ $24 - 10 =$ _____

Bo has _____ markers.   Mo has _____ markers.

8 **Subtract tens.**

Draw 5, 6, 7, 8, or 9 tens. Complete the problem using your number.

There are _____ shapes. 30 of them are squares. The rest are circles. How many are circles? Show your work.

_____ shapes are circles.

Jack has 27 cards. Kim has 34 cards. Owen has 20 cards. Jack wants to compare the numbers of cards. He wants to trade some cards. What math questions could Jack ask could about the cards?

In this unit, you will learn to compare numbers and to add two-digit numbers. Then you will be able to solve problems like Jack's!

✓ **Self Check**

Check off the skills you know now. Then see how many more you can check off after each lesson!

I can:	Before this unit	After this unit
rename numbers as tens and ones.	☐	☐
compare two-digit numbers.	☐	☐
add tens to any number.	☐	☐
add tens and ones.	☐	☐
regroup to add two-digit numbers.	☐	☐

Explore It

How many cubes do you have?

My guess: _____ cubes

_____

_____ ten _____ ones

_____

_____ tens _____ ones

_____

_____ tens _____ ones

©Curriculum Associates, LLC   Copying is not permitted.

▶▶ Try It

Boom has 4 tens and 5 ones. Buzz has 3 tens and 15 ones. Draw to show how Boom and Buzz could have the same number of cubes.

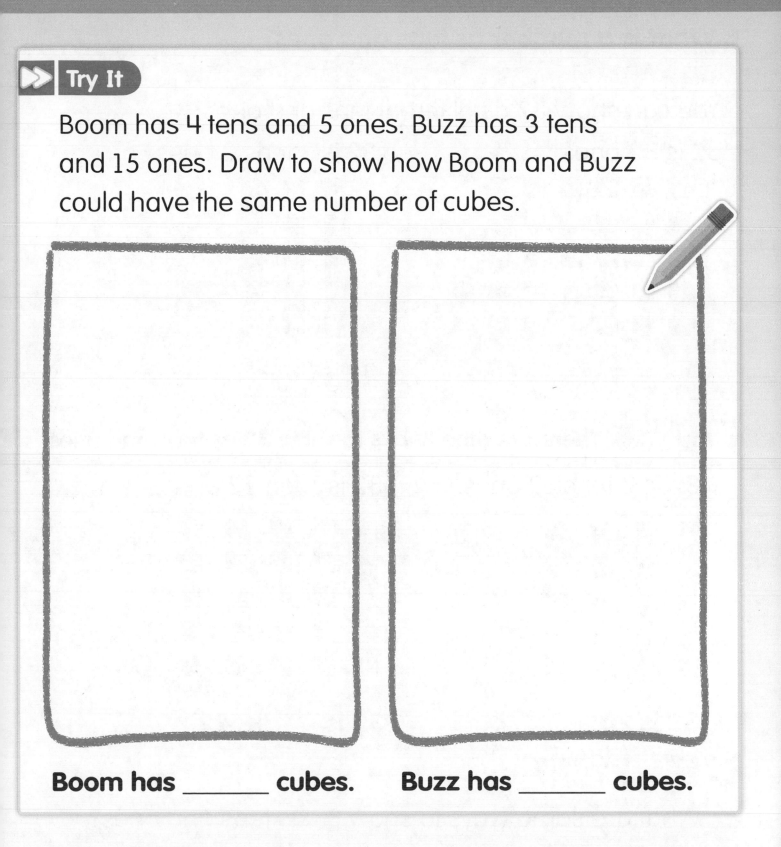

Boom has _____ cubes.   **Buzz has _____ cubes.**

Explore Together
Understand Tens and Ones

> **What is a number as tens and ones?**

You can show 32 as different tens and ones.

32 is 32 ones.

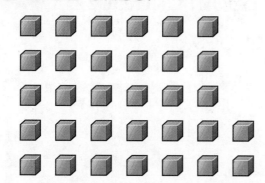

32 is 3 tens 2 ones.

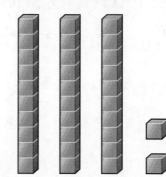

32 is 30 + 2.

Think There are other ways to show 32 as tens and ones.

32 is 2 tens 12 ones.

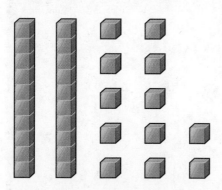

32 is 20 + ____.

32 is 1 ten 22 ones.

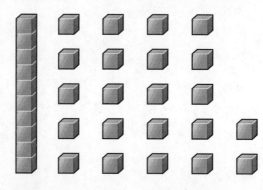

32 is ____ + 22.

Talk About It •

What are some ways to show 37 as tens and ones?

Understand Tens and Ones

 Show 23 as different tens and ones.
Use base-ten blocks.

Make 23 one way. ➔ Make 23 another way.

Write the tens and ones. Write the tens and ones.

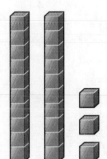

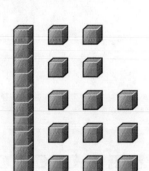

__2__ tens __3__ ones   __1__ ten __13__ ones

1 **Show 45 as tens and ones two ways.**

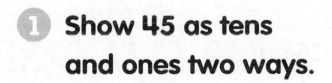

____ tens ____ ones

____ tens ____ ones

2 **Show 54 as tens and ones two ways.**

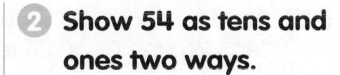

____ tens ____ ones

____ tens ____ ones

 Talk About It •

What are other ways you can show these numbers?

Connect It
Understand Tens and Ones

3 **Draw** Show why 36 ones is the same as 3 tens 6 ones.

4 **Identify** Circle all the ways that show 76.

7 tens 6 ones   6 tens 7 ones

60 + 7   70 + 6

5 tens 26 ones   6 tens 16 ones

5 **Explain** Buzz says 5 tens 8 ones = 5 + 80. Do you agree? Tell why or why not.

Show What I Know
Understand Tens and Ones

6 **Think about how you can show numbers as different tens and ones.**

A: Circle some tens and ones.

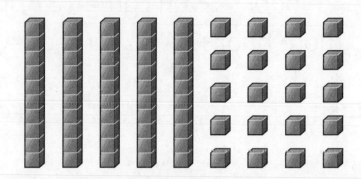

Write the number as tens and ones in two different ways. Write the two-digit number.

____ tens ____ ones   ____ tens ____ ones   ____

B: Use the two digits from A. Write a different number. Show this number as tens and ones in two different ways.

G | **Explore It**

Rosa carried 24 books. Ryan carried 37 books.
Who carried more books? Who carried fewer?

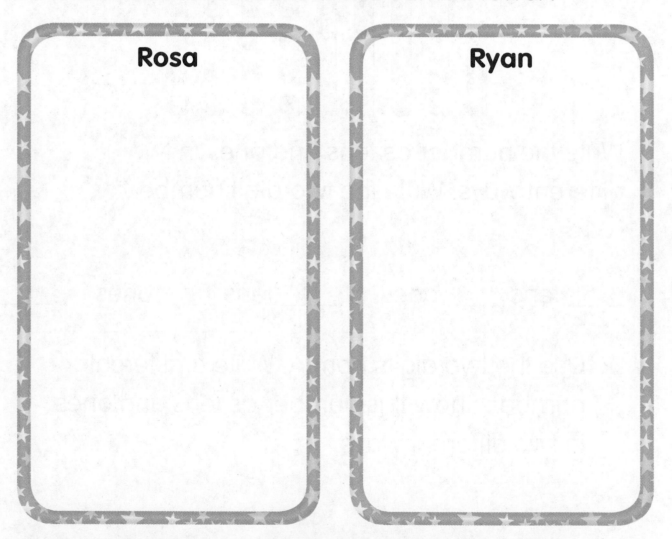

Rosa

Ryan

Ryan carried more / fewer books than Rosa.

Rosa carried more / fewer books than Ryan.

>> **Try It**

There are 28 soccer balls. There are 31 footballs.
Draw to compare the number of balls.

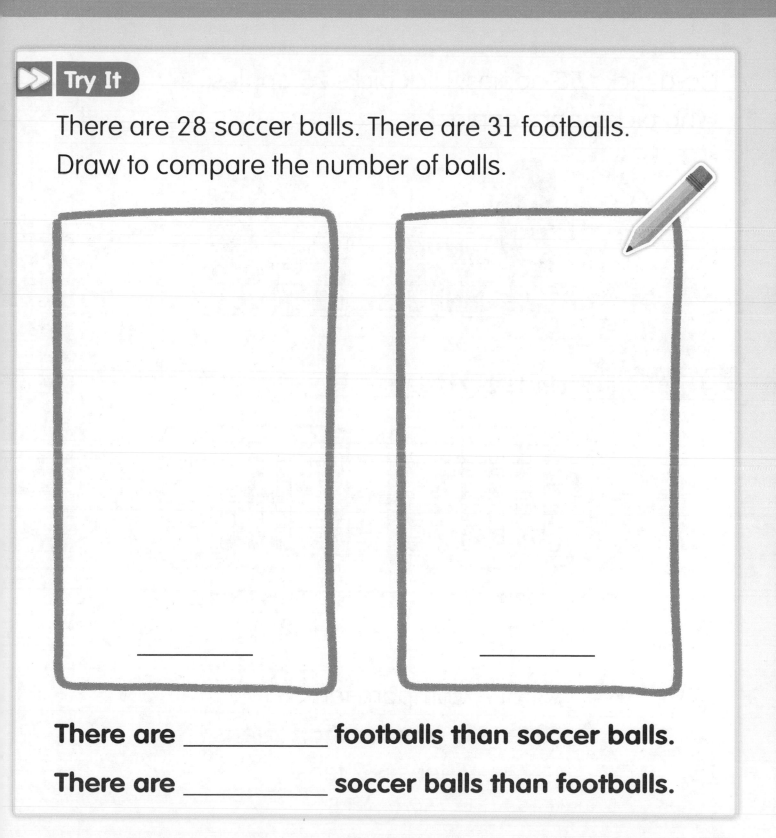

There are _____ footballs than soccer balls.

There are _____ soccer balls than footballs.

Compare Numbers

Nora picks 52 apples. Nick picks 25 apples.
Who picks more apples?

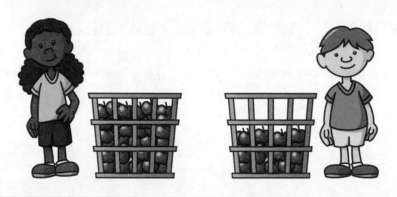

 **Model It**   Find 52 ? 25. •

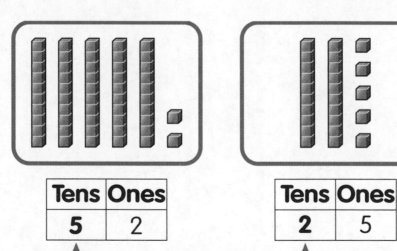

Tens	Ones
5	2

Tens	Ones
2	5

Compare tens.

5 tens **is greater than** 2 tens

5 tens > 2 tens

52 ◯ 25

Learn Together
Compare Numbers

Gabe collects 35 rocks.
Rose collects 39 rocks.
Who collects fewer rocks?

 **Model It** Find 35 (?) 39. •

Compare tens.
Tens are the same.
Compare ones.

Tens	Ones
3	**5**

Tens	Ones
3	**9**

5 ones **is less than** 9 ones

5 ones < 9 ones

35 ◯ 39

5 ◯ 9

 Talk About It Do you agree? Why or why not? • • • • • • • • • • • •

Fred collects 35 rocks.
Buzz says Fred collects more rocks than Gabe.

Compare Numbers

Jen has 48 coins. Kim has 14 coins.
Who has more coins?

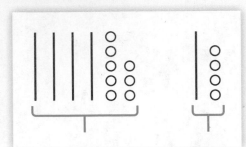

48   **14**

__4__ tens is greater than __1__ ten

48 **14**

---

1 Fill in the blanks, then write <, >, or = in the circle.

____ tens ____ ones   ____ tens ____ ones

72 ◯ **72**

---

2 Write <, >, or = in the circle.

23 ◯ **27**

Practice by Myself
Compare Numbers

3 Fill in the blanks, then write <, >, or = in the circle.

_____ tens _____ ones   _____ tens _____ ones

93 ◯ 48

4 Fill in the blanks, then write <, >, or = in the circle.

_____ tens _____ ones   _____ tens _____ ones

16 ◯ 60

5 Write <, >, or = in the circle.

42 ◯ 45

29 ◯ 29

50 ◯ 36

 **Explore It**

Maria has 17 shells. She finds 20 more.
How many shells does Maria have now?

___ + ___ = ___

Maria has _____ shells.

 **Try It**

Jordan has 13 toy cars and 10 toy trucks.
How many toys does Jordan have?

_____ + _____ = _____

Jordan has _____ toys.

Add Tens to Any Number

Eli has 16 red fish
and 10 yellow fish.
How many fish in all?

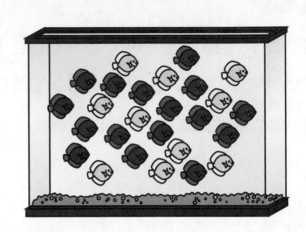

Model It Find 16 + 10.

Add the tens.

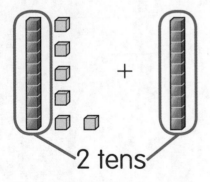

2 tens

10 + 10 = _____

Then add the ones.

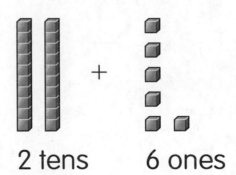

2 tens   6 ones

20 + 6 = _____

16 + 10 = _____

©Curriculum Associates, LLC   Copying is not permitted.

Learn Together
Add Tens to Any Number

50 blue balloons
and 13 red balloons.

How many balloons altogether?

Model It **Find 50 + 13.**

Write the tens and ones.

50 + □ 13 □

□ 10 □   □ 3 □

(50 + 10) + 3

Add the tens.
Then add the ones.

50 + 10 = 60

60 + ____ = ____

50 + 13 = ____

Talk About It **What is wrong?**

20 baseballs and 12 footballs. How many balls?

What's wrong?   2 + 10 + 2 = 14

▶ Show the right way.   ____ + ____ + ____ = ____

Add Tens to Any Number

10 blue marbles and 19 green marbles.
How many marbles in all?

10 + 10 = <u>20</u>

20 + 9 = <u>29</u>

10 + 19 = <u>29</u>

1 20 black cars and 32 white cars.
What is the total number of cars?

20 + 32 = ____

2 29 small ants and 10 big ants.
How many ants are there?

____ = 29 + 10

Practice by Myself
Add Tens to Any Number

3 70 small paper clips
and 14 big paper clips.
How many paper clips?

_____ = 70 + 14

4 40 green frogs and 25 yellow frogs.
How many frogs?

40 + 25 = _____

5 17 triangles and 20 squares.
How many shapes?

17 + 20 = _____

Add Tens and Add Ones

G | **Explore It**

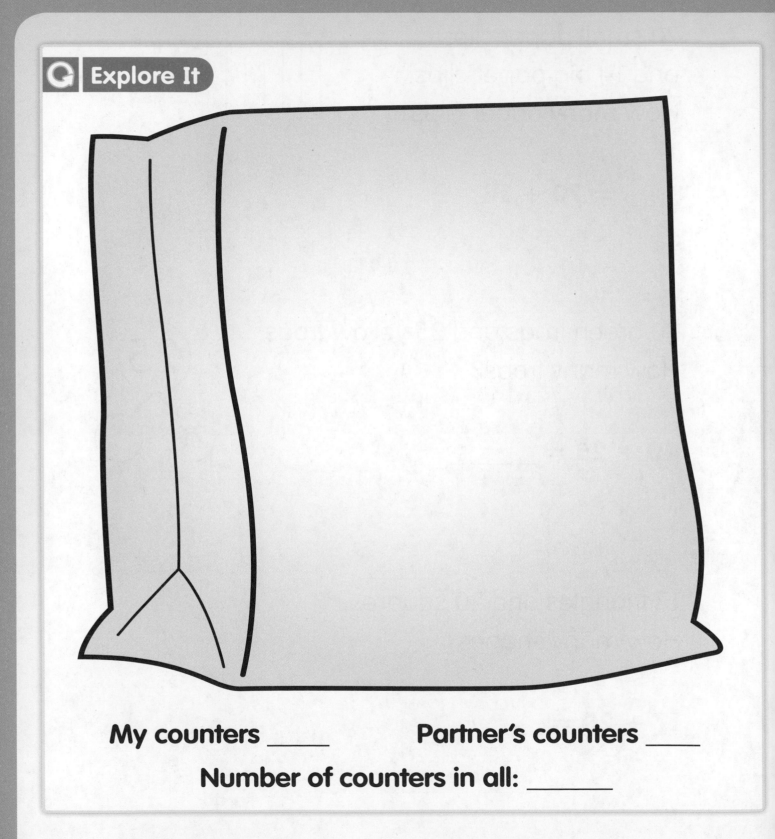

My counters _____   Partner's counters _____

Number of counters in all: _____

>> Try It

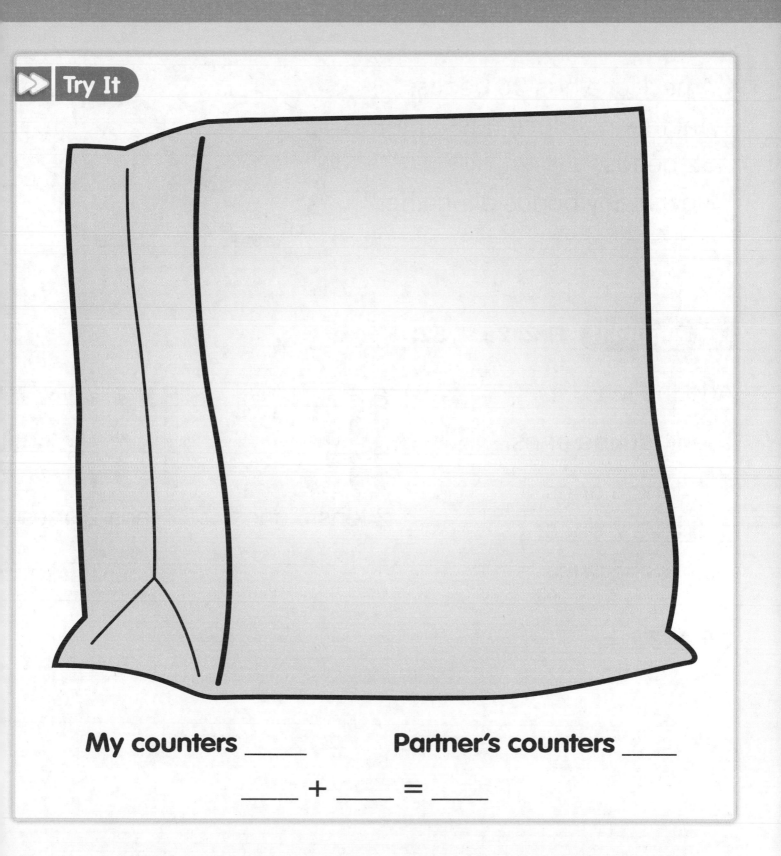

My counters _____   **Partner's counters** _____

_____ + _____ = _____

Add Tens and Add Ones

A necklace has 26 beads.
Another necklace has
32 beads.
How many beads altogether?

Model It Find 26 + 32. ·

Add the tens.

Then add the ones.

   2 tens 6 ones
+ 3 tens 2 ones
   5 tens 8 ones = ____

26 + 32 = ____

2 tens 6 ones   +   3 tens 2 ones

Learn Together
Add Tens and Add Ones

How many shells?

13 shells

14 shells

▣ Model It Find 13 + 14. •

Add the tens.
Then add the ones.

10 + 3
10 + 4
‾‾‾‾‾‾‾
20 + 7 = ____

13 + 14 = ____

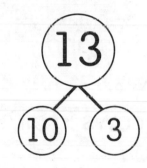
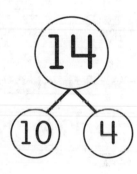

💬 Talk About It Who is right? How do you know? • • • • • • • • • •

Boom: 2 tens 5 ones
        + 1 ten   3 ones
        ‾‾‾‾‾‾‾‾‾‾‾‾‾‾
         3 tens 8 ones

Buzz: 20 + 5
      10 + 3
      ‾‾‾‾‾‾‾
      30 + 8

Practice Together
Add Tens and Add Ones

34 big beads and 55 small beads.
How many beads?

$30 + 4$

$50 + 5$

$\boxed{80} + \boxed{9} = \boxed{89}$

34 + 55 = <u>89</u>

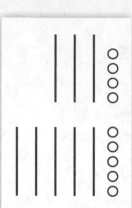

---

1 47 brown cows and
12 black cows.
How many cows in all?

$40 + \boxed{}$

$\boxed{} + 2$

$\boxed{} + \boxed{} = \boxed{}$

47 + 12 = _____

---

2 17 green pencils and
21 yellow pencils.
How many pencils?

_____ **= 17 + 21**

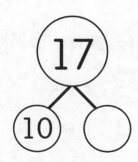

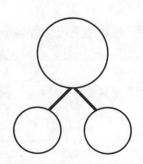

Practice by Myself
Add Tens and Add Ones

3 52 oak trees
and 35 pine trees.
How many trees in all?

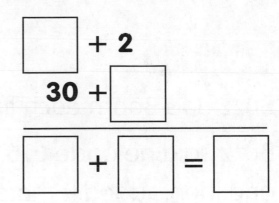

52 + 35 = _____

4 Manny has 43 cards.
Mark has 17 cards.
What is the total
number of cards?

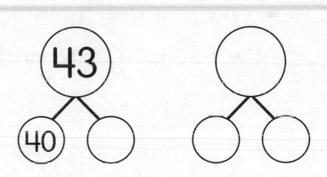

43 + 17 = _____

5 31 green grapes and 23 red grapes.
How many grapes altogether?

31 + 23 = _____

G **Explore It**

Buzz and Boom each find 16 + 8.

Buzz said he added 16 + 4 to make 20 and then added 4 more.

Boom said he broke 16 into 10 and 6. He added 6 + 4 to make ten, added 4 more, and then added the other ten. Show each strategy. Find each sum.

Buzz's sum: _____   **Boom's sum:** _____

>> **Try It**

Draw a picture to show how to find 17 + 5.

17 + 5 = _____

Add and Regroup

Lou has some erasers.
18 are blue. 7 are red.
How many erasers in all?

Model It   **Find 18 + 7.**

Make the next ten.

$$18 + 7$$

Then add the tens and ones.

$$18 + 2 + 5$$

$$20 + 5$$

$20 + 5 =$ _____

$18 + 7 =$ _____

Learn Together
Add and Regroup

How many marbles?

35 marbles

27 marbles

Model It **Find 35 + 27.** ••

Add the tens and ones.

5 tens   12 ones

50   +   12

50   +   10 + 2 = ____

35 + 27 = ____

Talk About It **Who is right? How do you know?** ••••••••••

Buzz: 25 + 16 = 41   Boom: 25 + 16 = 31

Practice Together
Add and Regroup

27 flower stickers. 64 star stickers.
How many stickers?

2 tens 7 ones
+ 6 tens 4 ones

8 tens 11 ones = 80   +   11

80   + 10 + 1

27 + 64 = _91_

---

1 38 soccer balls and 46 kickballs.
How many balls?

_____ **= 38 + 46**

---

2 17 yellow flowers and 28 white flowers.
How many flowers altogether?

17 + 28 = _____

1 ten   7 ones
+ 2 tens 8 ones

_____ tens _____ ones

Practice by Myself
Add and Regroup

3 33 math books and 27 reading books.
What is the total number of books?

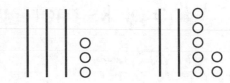

33 + 27 = ____

4 48 circles and 35 squares.
How many shapes?

____ = **48 + 35**

             4 tens 8 ones
        + 3 tens 5 ones

        ____ tens ____ ones

5 17 gold stars and 29 silver stars.
How many stars in all?

17 + 29 = ____

Unit 5 Review

Solve the problems.

1 Ali picks 73 pears.
Greg picks 37 pears.
Who picks more pears?

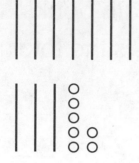

73 $\bigcirc$ 37

_____ picks more pears.

---

2 25 pink shells.
34 brown shells.
How many shells in all?

25 + 34 = ____

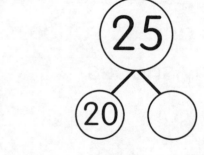
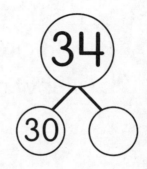

---

3 Circle ways to show 38.

3 tens 8 ones   30 + 8

80 + 3   2 tens 18 ones

4 20 + 51 = ____

---

5 Write <, >, or = in the circle.

54 $\bigcirc$ 56   19 $\bigcirc$ 19

6 ____ = 45 + 23

---

7 42 red birds. 46 blue birds.

Are there fewer red birds or blue birds?

Write the tens and ones.

Then write <, >, or = in the circle.

Tens	Ones

Tens	Ones

42 ◯ 46

There are _____ red birds than blue birds.

---

8 27 circles and 29 triangles.

How many shapes in all?

```
   2 tens 7 ones
+  2 tens 9 ones
```

_____ tens _____ ones

_____ = 27 + 29

There are _____ shapes in all.

Put It Together

9 **Add two numbers.**

Use the digits 5 and 7 to write a number.
Add your number to 28.
Show your work.

Eve has some shapes. She wants to put shapes together to make a new shape. She wants to make equal parts. What math questions could Eve ask about the shapes?

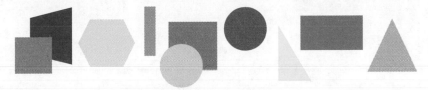

In this unit, you will learn about shapes and about equal parts of shapes. Then you will be able to solve problems like Eve's.

✓ **Self Check**

Check off the skills you know now. Then see how many more you can check off after each lesson!

I can:	Before this unit	After this unit
use sides and corners to name shapes.	☐	☐
put shapes together to make new shapes.	☐	☐
break shapes into halves.	☐	☐
break shapes into fourths.	☐	☐

Use What You Know
Understand Shapes

G | **Explore It**

Sort shapes.

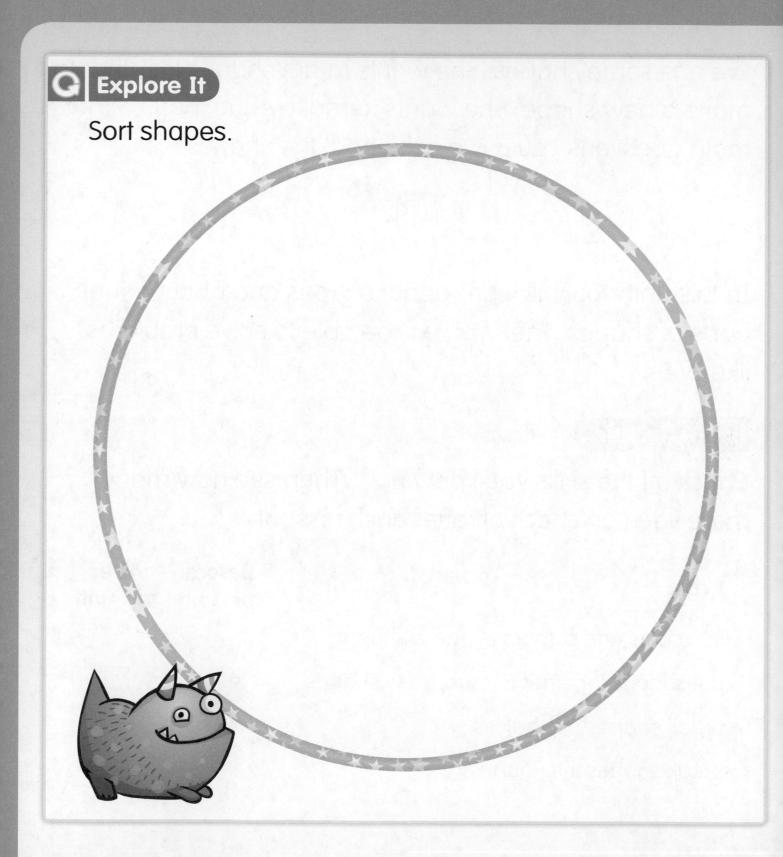

▶▶ **Try It**

Draw 3 shapes that are closed and have straight sides.

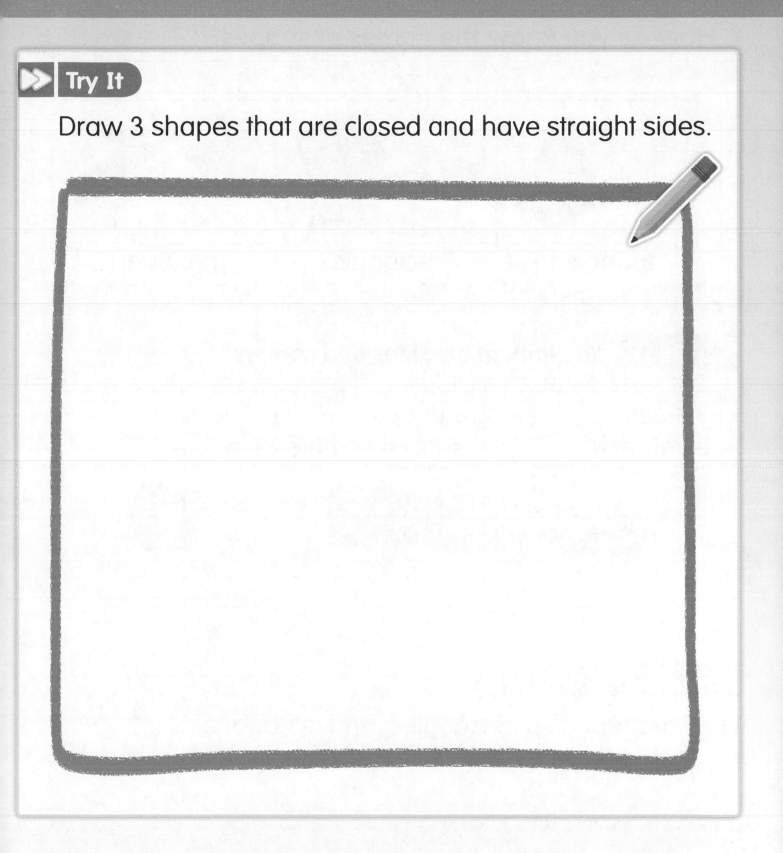

Explore Together
Understand Shapes

How do you know the names of shapes?

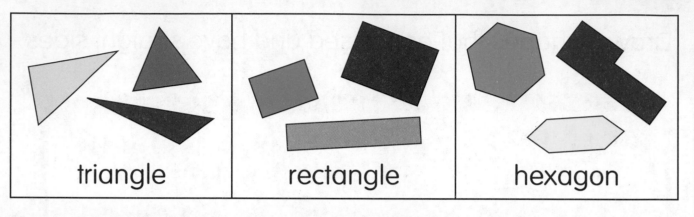

| triangle | rectangle | hexagon |

Think You look at the sides and corners. • • • • • • • • • • • • • • •

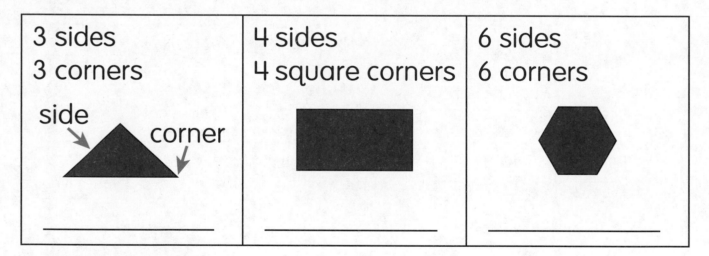

3 sides
3 corners

side   corner

_____

4 sides
4 square corners

_____

6 sides
6 corners

_____

Talk About It •

How are triangles, rectangles, and hexagons alike?
How are they different?

Understand Shapes

 Sort shapes with 4 sides and 4 corners.

Make a dot • ➡ Describe these rectangles.
if true.

Make an **X**
if not true.

X 4 sides the same length

• 4 square corners

• opposite sides the same length

---

1 **Describe these squares.**

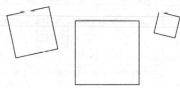

__ 4 sides the same length

__ 4 square corners

__ opposite sides the
same length

2 **Describe these rhombuses.**

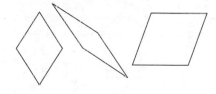

__ 4 sides the same length

__ 4 square corners

__ opposite sides the
same length

 Talk About It •

How are these shapes alike? How are they different?

Connect It
Understand Shapes

3 **Classify** Color the shapes.

triangles ■ hexagons ■ rectangles ■ rhombuses ■

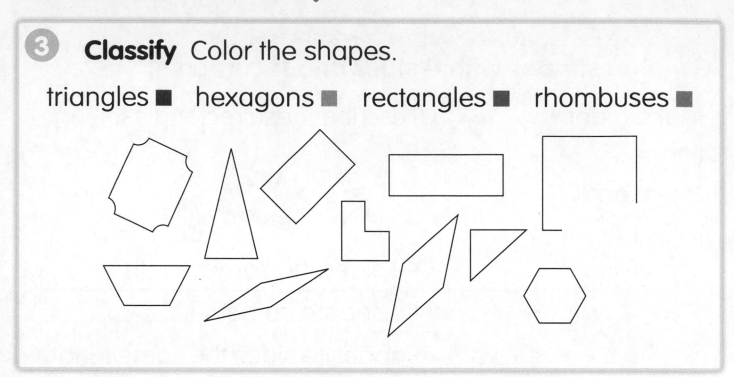

4 **Create** Draw the shape named in each box.

rhombus	trapezoid	square

5 **Evaluate** Eve says this shape is a rectangle.
Do you agree?
Why or why not?

Understand Shapes

6 **Make the same shape in different ways.**

A: Choose a shape to draw. Circle its name.

hexagon   triangle   rectangle
rhombus   square   trapezoid

Draw 3 of your shapes. Make each one
different in some way.

B: How are your shapes different? How are they alike?

Understand Putting Shapes Together

ⓖ Explore It

Make shapes.

>> **Try It**

Use 3 different shapes to make a hexagon.
Then trace the shapes you used.

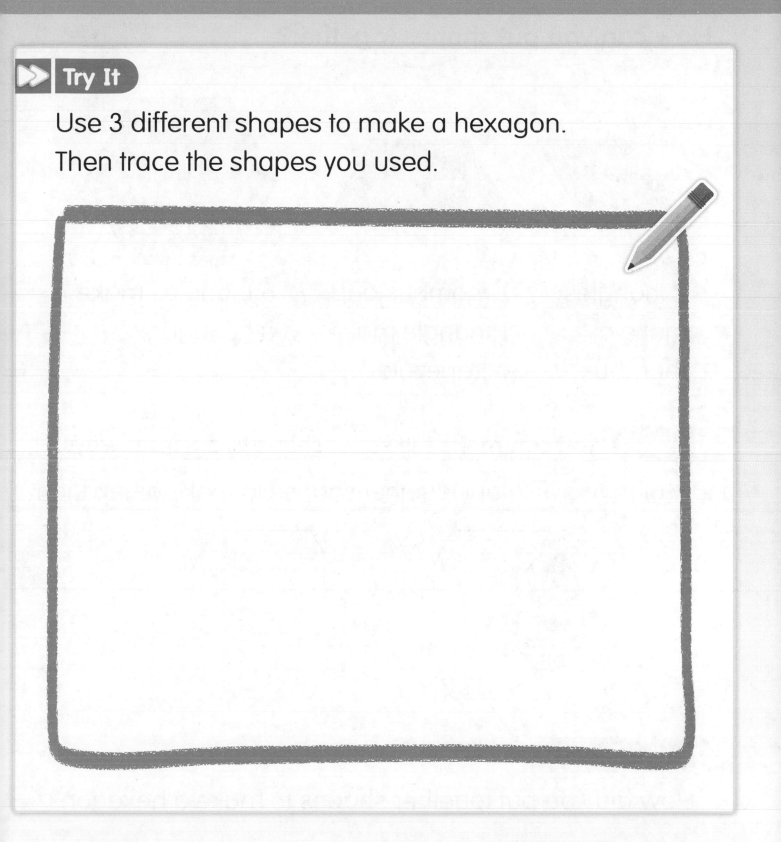

Understand Putting Shapes Together

How can you put shapes together?

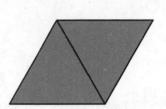

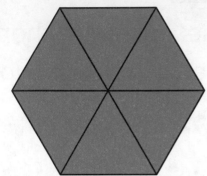

2 triangles make a rhombus

1 rhombus and 1 triangle make a trapezoid

6 triangles make a hexagon

 Think **You can make the same shape in different ways.**

Show other ways to put together shapes to make a hexagon.

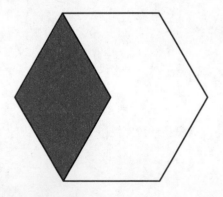
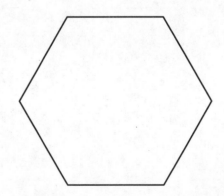

 Talk About It ·

How did you put together shapes to make a hexagon?

Understand Putting Shapes Together

✋ **Put together shapes to make new shapes.**

Use shapes. → Put shapes together. Trace each shape. → Make a new shape. Trace each shape.

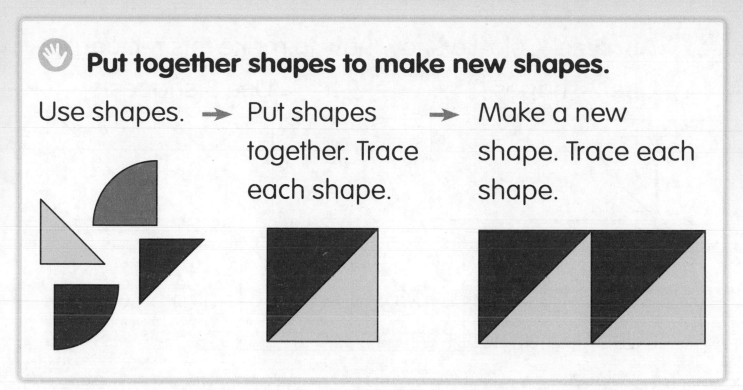

---

1 **Make this.**

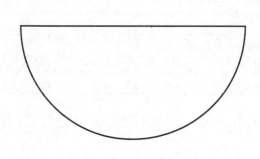

2 **Then make this.**

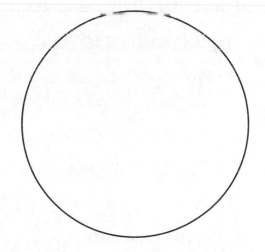

💬 **Talk About It** •

What other shapes can you make with shape pieces?

Understand Putting Shapes Together

3 **Analyze** Color to show how to make this rectangle.

Use 2 shapes.   Use 3 shapes.

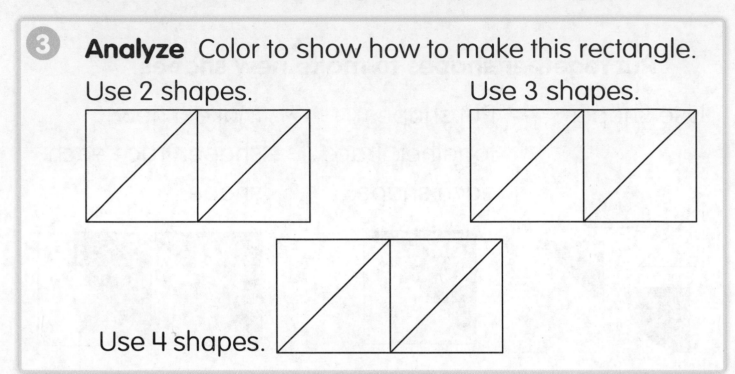

Use 4 shapes.

4 **Create** Use the shapes from Problem 3 to make a trapezoid. Draw it.

5 **Evaluate** Buzz says the 2 triangles make a square. Boom says the shape is not a square. Who is right? How do you know?

Understand Putting Shapes Together

6 **Think about how to put shapes together.**

A: Use 4 or more shapes to make 2 new shapes. Draw them.

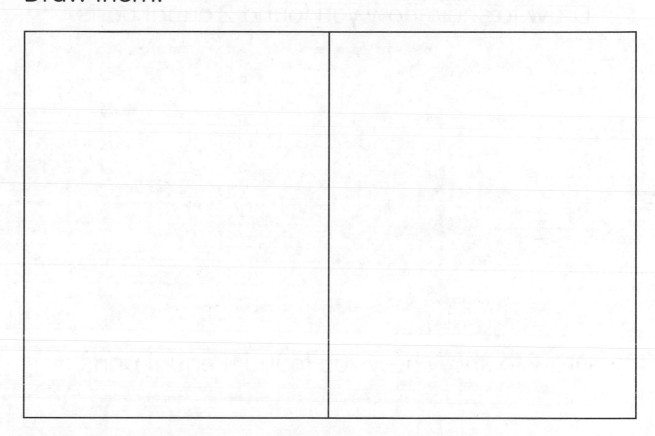

B: Circle one shape above. Write how many of each shape you used.

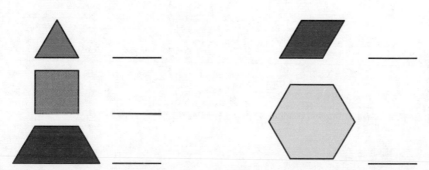

G | **Explore It**

Draw to show how you found 2 equal parts.

Draw to show how you found 4 equal parts.

>> **Try It**

Draw to show how you found 4 equal parts.

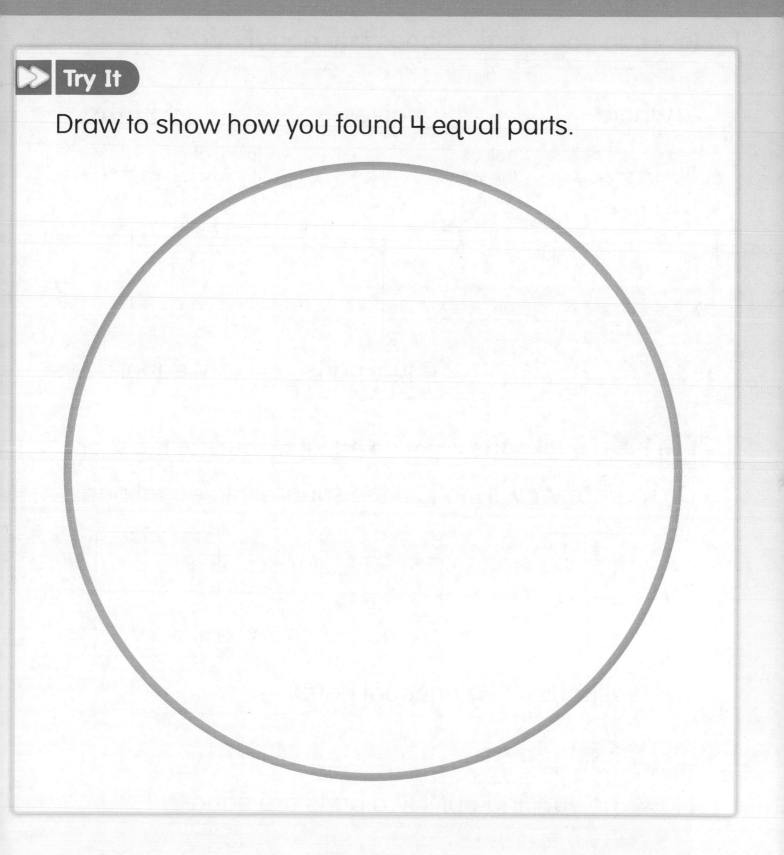

Understand Breaking Shapes into Parts

How can you break shapes into equal parts?

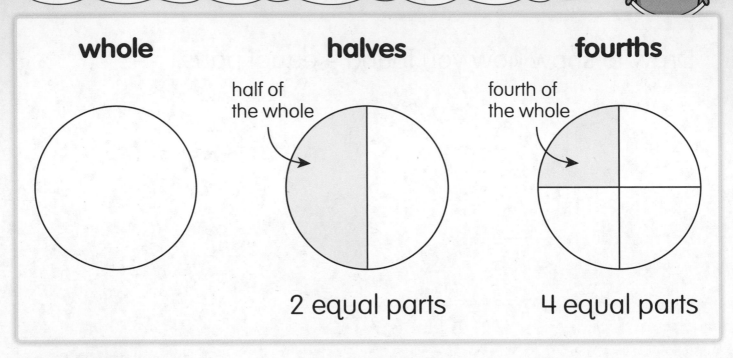

| whole | halves | fourths |

half of the whole

fourth of the whole

2 equal parts   4 equal parts

Think **Equal parts cover an equal amount of the shape.**

Draw another way to fold the square into equal parts.

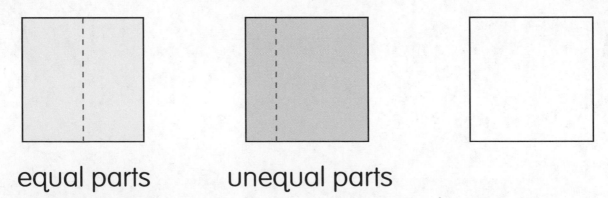

equal parts   unequal parts

Talk About It •

How can you find out if two parts are equal?

©Curriculum Associates, LLC   Copying is not permitted.

Understand Breaking Shapes into Parts

 Fold shapes into equal parts.

Fold each → Draw equal → Circle the word that
shape.   parts.   describes the parts.

 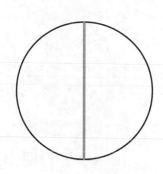

(halves)

fourths

---

1 Draw 4 equal parts.

halves

fourths

2 Draw 4 equal parts.

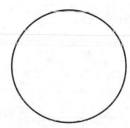

halves

quarters

 **Talk About It** ·

Look at a half of a circle. Look at a fourth of the same circle.
Which part is larger?

Understand Breaking Shapes into Parts

3 **Explain** Jake's pizza is cut into 2 equal pieces. Kim's pizza is cut into 4 equal pieces. Which pieces are smaller? Show how you know.

 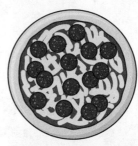

Jake's pizza   Kim's pizza

4 **Identify** Write how many equal parts.

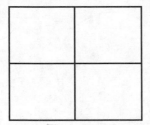

_____ equal parts

5 **Analyze** Buzz says that he shaded a quarter of this shape. Do you agree? Why or why not?

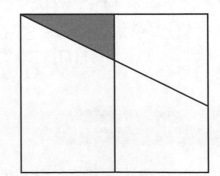

Show What I Know
Understand Breaking Shapes into Parts

6 **Think about breaking shapes into equal parts.**

A: Ben has these cookies.

He shares the cookies with a friend.
They each get equal parts.
Color what Ben gets.

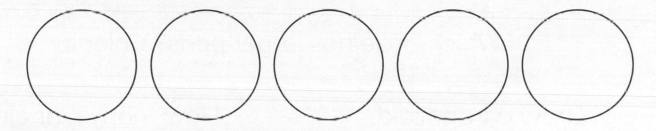

B: 4 friends share the cookies.
Color what Ben gets.

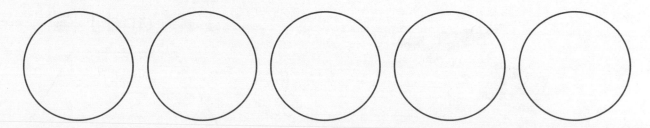

Solve the problems.

1 How many equal parts are there?

____ equal parts

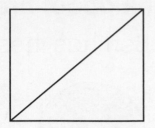

---

2 This circle shows

_____.

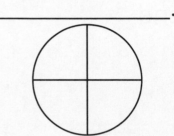

This circle shows

_____.

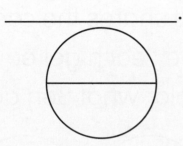

Which circle has larger parts? Color it.

---

3 Draw a trapezoid.

4 How many triangles?

____

---

5 Circle the rectangle.

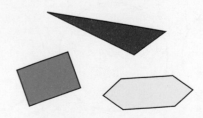

6 Break the shape into 1 ◢ and 1 ▲.

What shape is this? _____

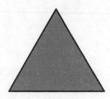

Put two of these shapes together. Draw.
What shape do they make?

The two _____ make a _____.

---

8 Circle the words that describe a rhombus.

3 sides

4 sides the same length

1 square corner

opposite sides the same length

6 sides

Put It Together

9 **Make shapes.**

Put together 2 or 4 triangles like this ◣.

Make a shape with 4 sides. Describe the shape.

The shape is a _____.
It has _____ equal parts.

Circle the word that describes
the equal parts.

halves   fourths.

Use the shape you made.
Add some other shapes
to make a new shape.

Draw the new shape.

How Many? How Much? How Long?

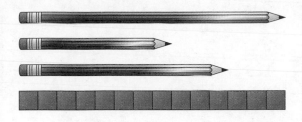

Sara has pencils of different lengths. She wants to know the lengths of the pencils. What math questions could Sara ask about the pencils?

In this unit, you will learn how to sort objects, tell time, and measure length. Then you will be able to solve problems like Sara's.

✓ Self Check

Check off the skills you know now. Then see how many more you can check off after each lesson!

I can:	Before this unit	After this unit
sort and count objects.	☐	☐
compare data.	☐	☐
order objects by length.	☐	☐
compare lengths of objects.	☐	☐
measure lengths of objects.	☐	☐
tell time to the hour and half-hour.	☐	☐

Use What You Know
Sort and Count

G Explore It

How can you sort the cubes?

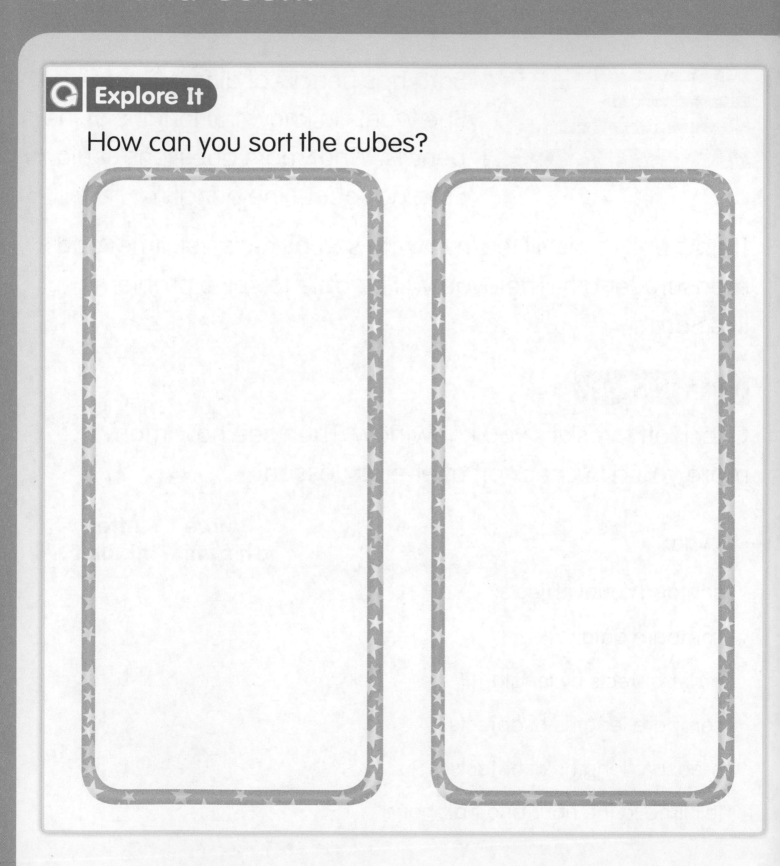

Try It

How can you sort the fish?

Sort and Count

What shapes are there? How many of each shape?

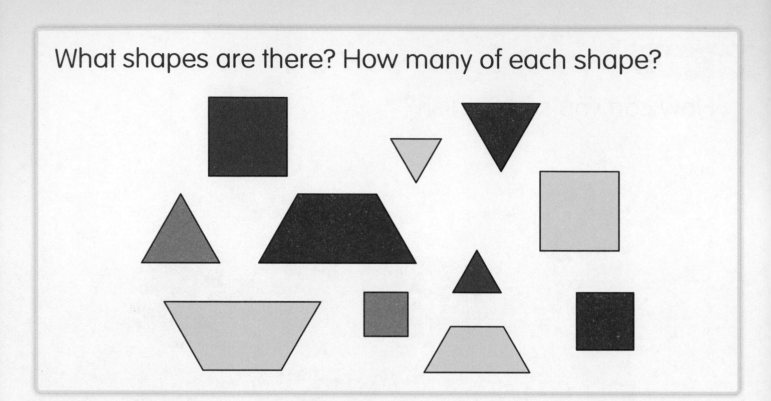

 Model It Make a chart. ●●●●●●●●●●●●●●●●●●●●●●●●●●●●●●

Sort by shape. You can make a tally chart to count.

You can also make a chart with numbers.

Shapes	How Many
△	IIIII
□	
⬭	

Shapes	How Many
△	
□	
⬭	

Learn Together
Sort and Count

What color are the pencils?

How many of each color?

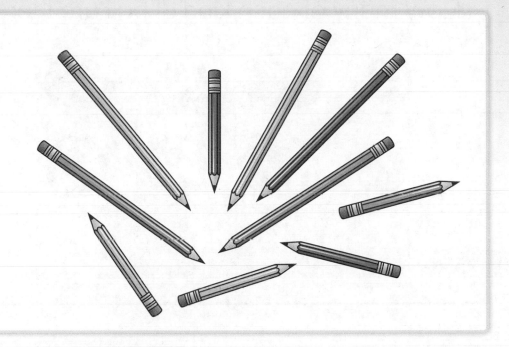

Model It Make a picture graph. ●●●●●●●●●●●●●●●●●●●●●

Sort and count.

Pencils	How Many
✏️	‖‖‖
✏️	
✏️	

Use circles to show how many.

Pencils	How Many
✏️	O O O O
✏️	
✏️	

Talk About It Do you agree? Why or why not? ●●●●●●●●●●●●

Buzz says he can sort the pencils by size.

Practice Together
Sort and Count

How many of each kind of ball are there?

You can make a tally chart.
You can make a picture graph.

1 Complete the tally chart.

Ball	How Many
🏈	IIII
⚫	
⚽	

2 Complete the picture graph.

Ball	How Many
🏈	O O O
⚫	
⚽	

Practice by Myself
Sort and Count

Use the data.

Favorite Fruit

3 Make a tally chart.

Favorite Fruit	How Many
🍎	
🍌	
🍐	

Make a chart with numbers.

Favorite Fruit	How Many
🍎	
🍌	
🍐	

4 Make a picture graph.

Favorite Fruit	How Many
🍎	
🍌	
🍐	

 **Explore It**

Make a picture graph.

Shape	Number of Shapes

What does the picture graph show?

▶▶ **Try It**

Write about the picture graph.

Number of responses in all _____

Shape with most responses _____

Shape with fewest responses _____

There are more _____ than squares.

A question I can ask about our picture graph is:

_____

_____

_____

_____.

Compare Data

Children name their pets. They make a picture graph with the data. How many have dogs or cats?

Our Pets

Bird	☺ ☺
Dog	☺ ☺ ☺ ☺ ☺ ☺ ☺
Cat	☺ ☺ ☺ ☺

▦ Model It **Find how many children have dogs or cats.**

Each picture shows 1 child. Count the pictures for dogs. Count the pictures for cats. Then add.

Our Pets

Bird	☺ ☺	
Dog	① ② ③ ④ ⑤ ⑥ ⑦	_____ dogs
Cat	① ② ③ ④	_____ cats

7 + 4 = _____

_____ children have dogs or cats.

Learn Together
Compare Data

How many more
🍐 than 🍎 ?

Favorite Fruits	How Many
🍐	14
🍌	8
🍎	12

▦ Model It

Color the squares to show how many.

14 is how many more than 12?

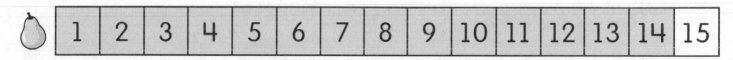

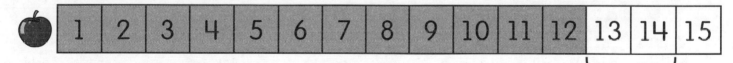

There are _____ more 🍐 than 🍎 .

💬 Talk About It

Look at the chart. What other questions can you ask?

What answers can you find?

Compare Data

Circle the fruit that the most children like.

Fruit	Number of Children
🍎	☺ ☺ ☺ ☺ ☺ ☺
🍓	☺ ☺ ☺ ☺ ☺
🍇	☺ ☺ ☺ ☺ ☺ ☺ ☺ ☺

1 Children counted their blocks. How many blocks did they count in all?

They counted _____ blocks in all.

Blocks	How Many
◆	9
▽	4
△	6

2 The tally chart shows Ms. Lee's markers.

Marker	Tally Marks
Blue	||||| ||||| ||
Red	||||| |||
Yellow	||||| ||||| |||||

How many more yellow than red? _____

How many fewer red than blue? _____

Practice by Myself
Compare Data

3 The tally chart shows what children like best.
Write the number for each object.
Circle the one that the most children like.

 ____

 ____

 ____

Object	Tally Marks
	IIII IIII II
	IIII III
	IIII IIII IIII III

4 Circle what more children like.
Write how many more.

 or ____ **more**

Circle what fewer children like.
Write how many fewer.

 or  ____ **fewer**

G **Explore It**

Which pencil is the shortest?

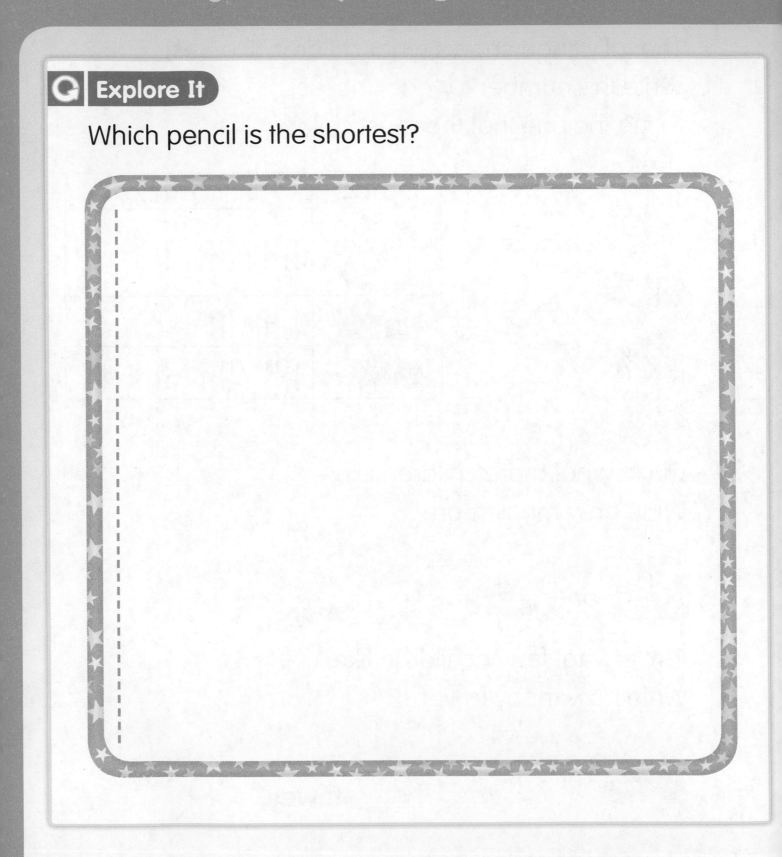

⏩ Try It

Which straw is the tallest?

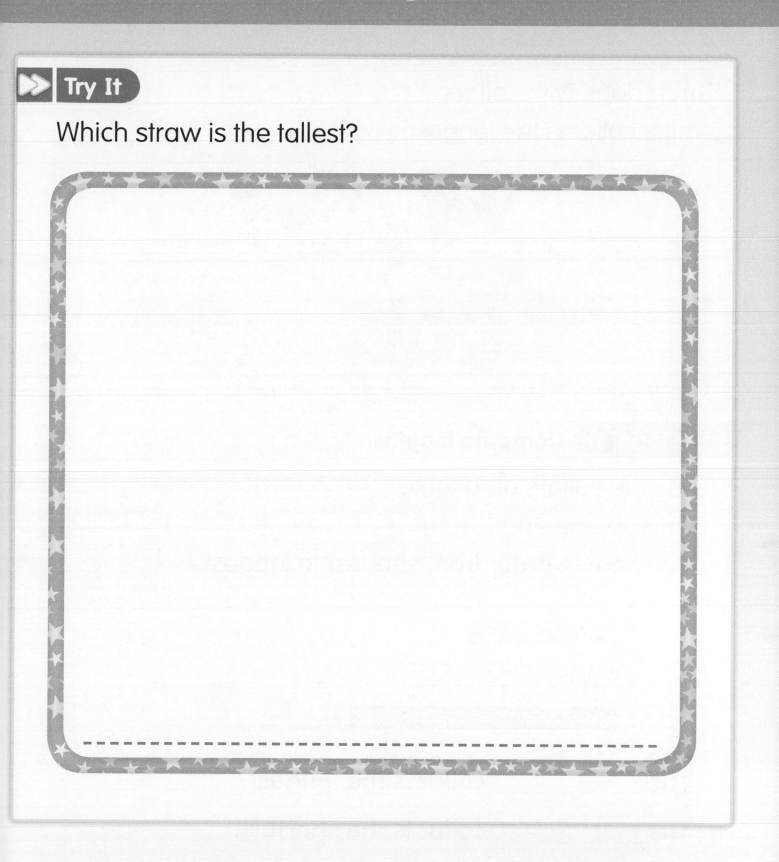

Order Objects by Length

Three dogs with collars.
Which collar is the longest?

Model It   **Compare lengths.** ·

Lay the collars on a table.

Line up one end.

Put them in order from shortest to longest.

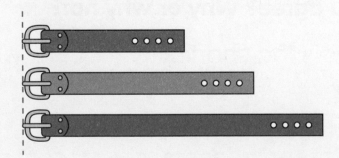

The _____ collar is the longest.

The _____ collar is the shortest.

Order Objects by Length

Ron puts books on a shelf.
He wants to order them
from shortest to tallest.
Which book is shortest?

Model It **Order the books from shortest to tallest.**

Stand the books on a shelf.
Circle the shortest.
Put an X on the tallest.

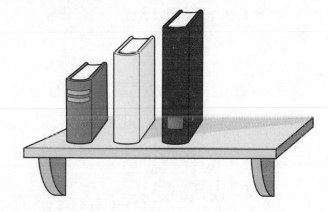

Talk About It **Do you agree? Why or why not?**

Boom says the red flower is the shortest.

Practice Together
Order Objects by Length

Color the worm that is the shortest.
The middle worm is longest.
The top worm is shorter than
the bottom worm.

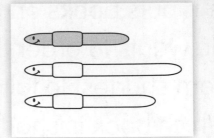

1 Draw lines to show
which pencil is longest
and which is shortest.

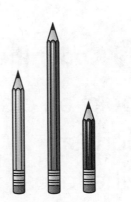

shortest   longest

2 Read the clues.
Then color the dogs.

The red dog is longest.

The blue dog is shorter
than the yellow dog.

Order Objects by Length

3 Read the clues.
Then color the bats.

The green bat is shortest.
The red bat is longer than
the blue bat.

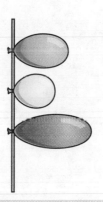

4 Circle the word that makes the
sentence true.

The green balloon is shorter / longer
than the orange balloon.

5 Draw a line that is taller than both rectangles.

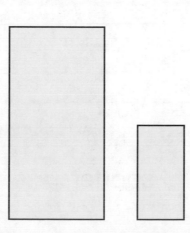

Ⓖ Explore It

Trace your strip next to the strip of paper below.
Is it taller, shorter, or the same? Circle the word.

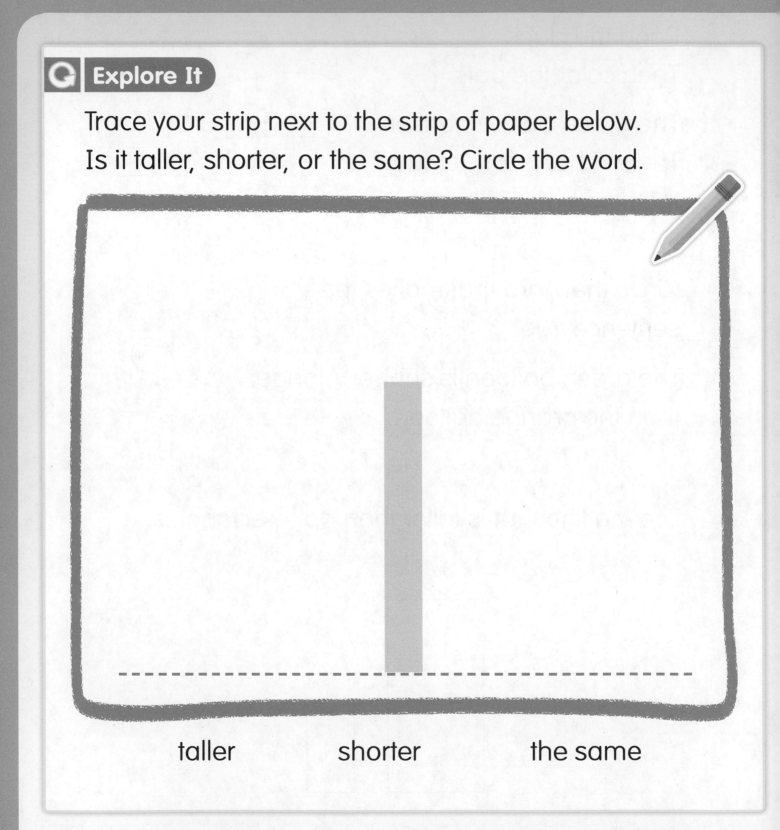

taller   shorter   the same

▶▶ **Try It**

Draw a line that is shorter than the first pencil.

Then draw a line that is longer than the second pencil.

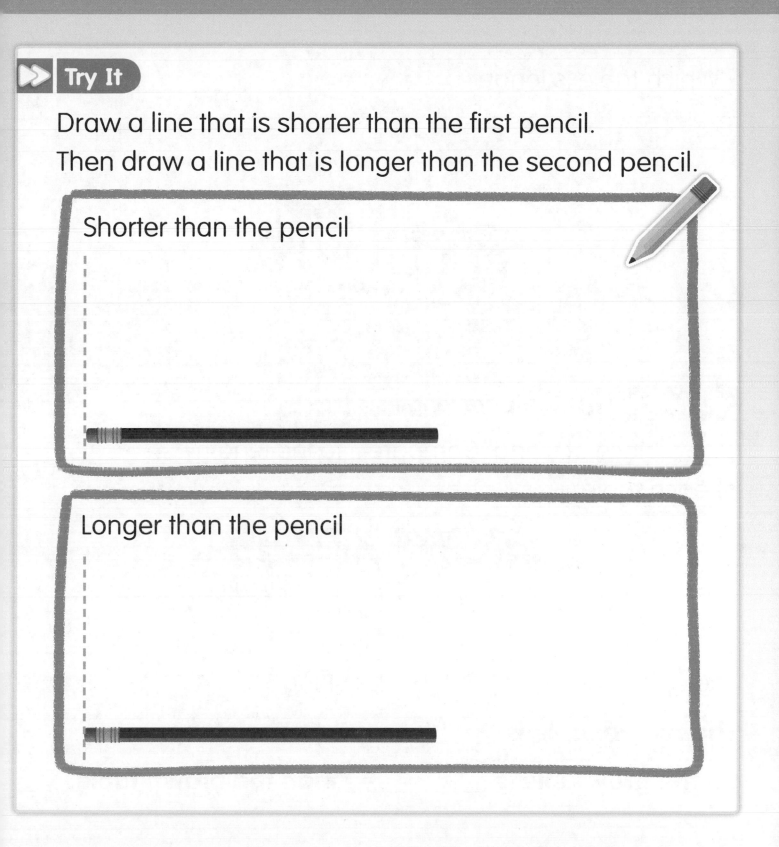

Shorter than the pencil

Longer than the pencil

Compare Lengths

Which table is longer?

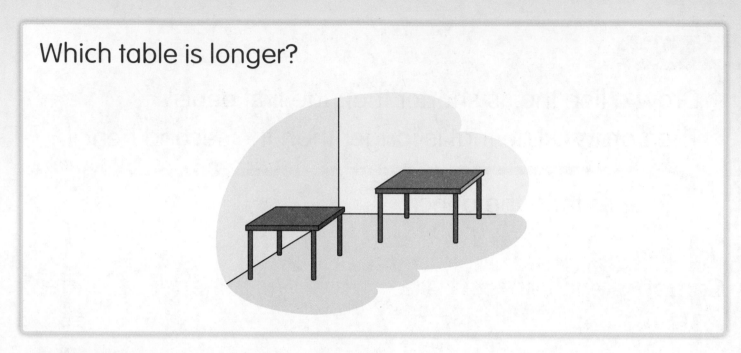

.:: **Model It** **Compare lengths.** •

Use a piece of string. Compare it to the length
of each table.

The gray table is longer than the string.

The brown table is _____ than the string.

So the gray table is _____ than the brown table.

Learn Together
Compare Lengths

Which object is shorter?

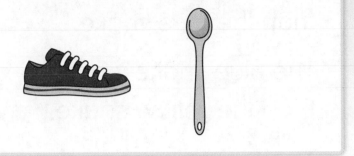

Model It **Use a paper strip.** ·

Compare each object to the paper. Write shorter or longer.

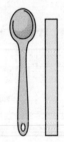

_____   _____

The shoe is _____ than the spoon.

Talk About It **Do you agree? Why or why not?** · · · · · · · · · · · ·

Chris is shorter than Amy.

Ray is taller than Amy.

Boom says Chris is taller than Ray.

Practice Together
Compare Lengths

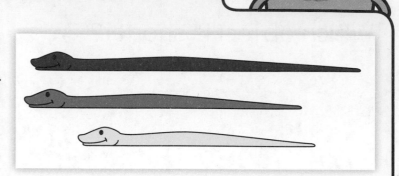

The red snake is longer than the blue snake.

The blue snake is longer than the yellow snake.

The _____red_____ **snake is the longest.**

---

1 Draw a line that is shorter than the triangle.
Circle the tallest object.

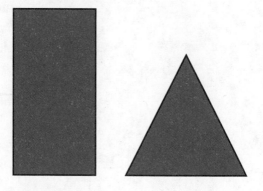

---

2 The crayon is shorter than the pencil.
The pencil is shorter than the notebook.

The crayon is _____ than the notebook.

Practice by Myself
Compare Lengths

3 Compare lengths.
Then circle the correct words.

is (longer than, shorter than) .

4 Draw a line that is taller than the star.
Which of the three pictures is tallest? Circle it.

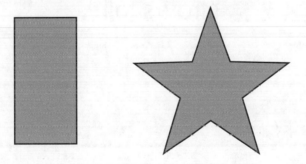

5 The bee is longer than the ant.
The worm is longer than the bee.

The ant is _____ than the worm.

G Explore It

Write the number of straws used to measure the height of each partner.

Name _____

about _____ straws tall

Name _____

about _____ straws tall

Who is taller? How do you know?

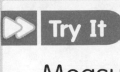 **Try It**

Measure the length of the string using straws.
Write how many straws long it is.

about _____ straw long

Understand Length Measurement

How do you measure length?

Length tells you how long an object is.
You can find the length of a pencil.

Length

Think You can use tiles to measure length.

Line up the edge of the first tile with the edge of the pencil.

Count the tiles.

There are 10 tiles.

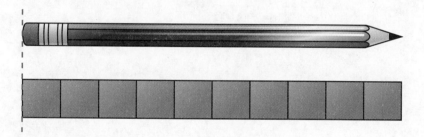

The pencil is _____ tiles long.

Talk About It

Do the tiles need to be the same size?
Why or why not?

Understand Length Measurement

✋ **Measure the length two ways.**

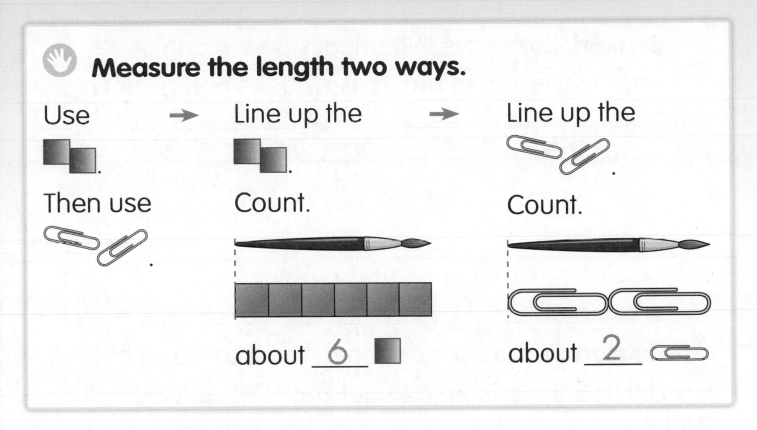

Use ➡ Line up the ➡ Line up the

Then use

Count.

Count.

about __6__ ▪

about __2__ ⌷

1 Measure the length two ways.

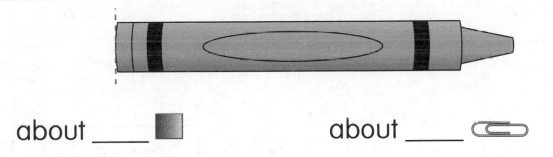

about ____ ▪   about ____ ⌷

💬 **Talk About It** ·

Do you need more ▪ or ⌷ to measure the crayon?
Why?

Connect It
Understand Length Measurement

2 **Explain** Buzz says this string is 8 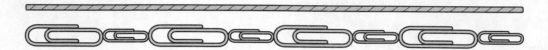 long. Boom says that is wrong. How does Boom know?

3 **Reason** Boom uses 8 squares to measure a ribbon. Did Boom measure the right way? Why or why not?

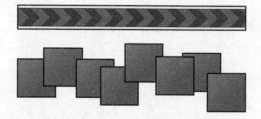

4 **Analyze** Boom says that his leaf is 4 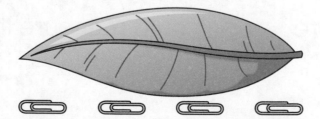 long. Do you agree? Why or why not?

Understand Length Measurement

5 **Think about measuring length.**

A: Use ■ and ■. Circle the correct answer.

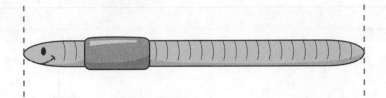

Does it take more ■ or more ■ to measure the worm?

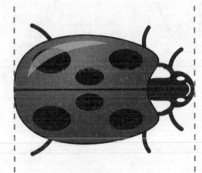

Does it take fewer ■ or fewer ■ to measure the ladybug?

B: Draw a pencil. Measure it with ■ and ■.

about _____ ■   about _____ ■

Use What You Know
Tell Time

Explore It

Show 4 o'clock.

Show 7 o'clock.

Show 10 o'clock.

Show 2 o'clock.

>> **Try It**

_____ o'clock

Tell Time

It is 2 o'clock.

Next, it is just past 2 o'clock.

Then it is almost 3 o'clock.

Where is the **hour hand** at each time?

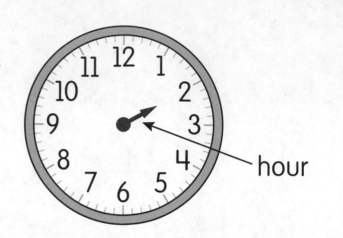

hour

Model It Show the hour hand. ················

Draw the **hour hand** to show the time.

2 o'clock

just past 2 o'clock

almost 3 o'clock

Tell Time

What time do these clocks show?

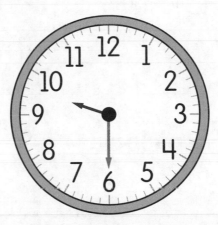

Model It **Read the time.** •

The **minute hand** is halfway around the clock.

The hour hand is halfway between 9 and 10.

It is half past _____.

It is 30 minutes after _____.

It is _____:30,
or nine thirty.

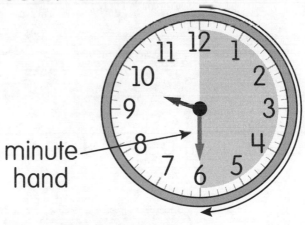

minute hand

Talk About It **Do you agree? Why or why not?** • • • • • • • • • •

Buzz says 9:30 is halfway between 9:00 and 10:00.
So, 30 minutes is the same as a half hour.

These clocks show the same time.

What time is it?

It is _7_ **o'clock.**

1 Circle the clock that shows 4:00.

2 It is half past 3. Draw the time on these clocks.

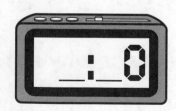 

Practice by Myself
Tell Time

3 Read the digital clock.
Draw the hands to
show the time.

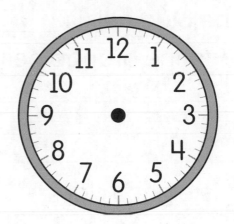

4 Circle the clock that shows 11:00.

5 It is eight thirty. Draw the times on these clocks.

Unit 7 Review

Solve the problems.

1 The blue belt is _____
than the orange belt.

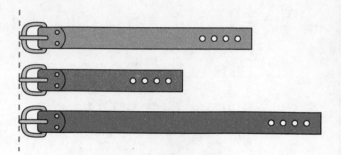

2 It is eight o'clock.
Show the time on
these clocks.

3 Make a tally chart and a chart with numbers.
Then fill in the blanks.

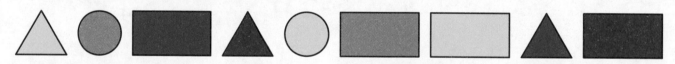

Shapes	How Many
△	
▭	
○	

Shapes	How Many
△	
▭	
○	

_____ more ▭ than ○   _____ fewer ○ than △

4 Read the clues.
Then color the dogs.

The blue dog is shortest.

The yellow dog is longer
than the red dog.

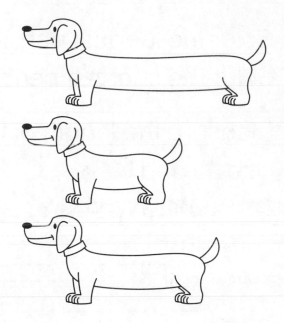

---

5 It is half past 7.

It is _____ minutes after _____ o'clock.

Show the time on these clocks.

Put It Together

6 **Compare and measure.**

Color the longest pencil red.
Color the shortest pencil blue.

Measure the length of the longest pencil.
Use 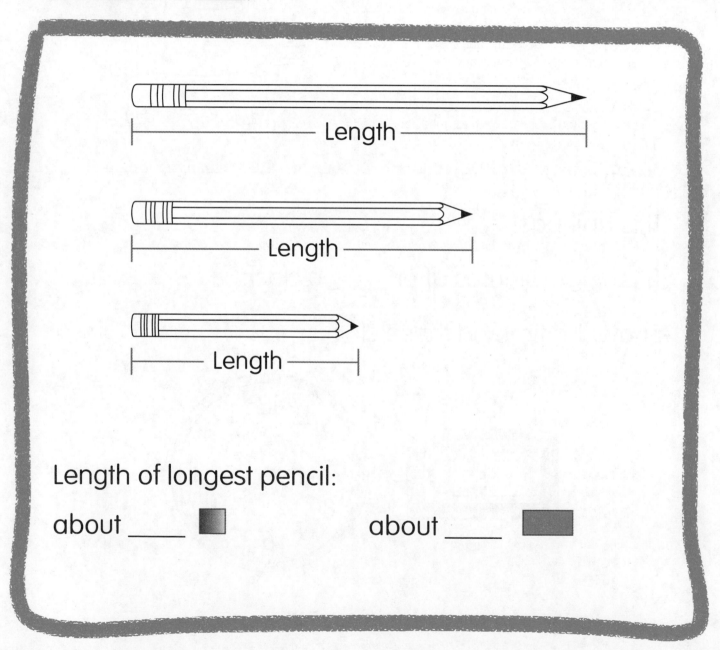 and .

Length

Length

Length

Length of longest pencil:

about ____   about ____

Common Core State Standards Coverage by *Ready* Instruction

The chart below correlates each Common Core State Standard to the *Ready® Instruction* lesson(s) that offer(s) comprehensive instruction on that standard. Use this chart to determine which lessons your students should complete based on their mastery of each standard.

Common Core State Standards for Grade 1 Mathematical Standards	Content Emphasis	*Ready* Common Core Instruction Lesson(s)
Operations and Algebraic Thinking		
Represent and solve problems involving addition and subtraction.		
1.OA.A.1 Use addition and subtraction within 20 to solve word problems involving situations of adding to, taking from, putting together, taking apart, and comparing, with unknowns in all positions, e.g., by using objects, drawings, and equations with a symbol for the unknown number to represent the problem.	Major	3, 5
1.OA.A.2 Solve word problems that call for addition of three whole numbers whose sum is less than or equal to 20, e.g., by using objects, drawings, and equations with a symbol for the unknown number to represent the problem.	Major	15
Understand and apply properties of operations and the relationship between addition and subtraction.		
1.OA.B.3 Apply properties of operations as strategies to add and subtract. *Examples: If 8 + 3 = 11 is known, then 3 + 8 = 11 is also known. (Commutative property of addition.) To add 2 + 6 + 4, the second two numbers can be added to make a ten, so 2 + 6 + 4 = 2 + 10 = 12. (Associative property of addition.)*	Major	8
1.OA.B.4 Understand subtraction as an unknown-addend problem. *For example, subtract 10 − 8 by finding the number that makes 10 when added to 8.*	Major	4
Add and subtract within 20.		
1.OA.C.5 Relate counting to addition and subtraction (e.g., by counting on 2 to add 2).	Major	1, 18
1.OA.C.6 Add and subtract within 20, demonstrating fluency for addition and subtraction within 10. Use strategies such as counting on; making ten (e.g., 8 + 6 = 8 + 2 + 4 = 10 + 4 = 14); decomposing a number leading to a ten (e.g., 13 − 4 = 13 − 3 − 1 = 10 − 1 = 9); using the relationship between addition and subtraction (e.g., knowing that 8 + 4 = 12, one knows 12 − 8 = 4); and creating equivalent but easier or known sums (e.g., adding 6 + 7 by creating the known equivalent 6 + 6 + 1 = 12 + 1 = 13).	Major	2, 6, 9, 11, 13, 14, 16

The Standards for Mathematical Practice are integrated throughout the instructional lessons.

Common Core State Standards ©2010. National Governors Association Center for Best Practices and Council of Chief State School Officers. All rights reserved.

Common Core State Standards for Grade 1 Mathematical Standards	Content Emphasis	*Ready*® Common Core Instruction Lesson(s)
Operations and Algebraic Thinking *continued*		
Work with addition and subtraction equations.		
1.OA.D.7 Understand the meaning of the equal sign, and determine if equations involving addition and subtraction are true or false. *For example, which of the following equations are true and which are false? 6 = 6, 7 = 8 − 1, 5 + 2 = 2 + 5, 4 + 1 = 5 + 2.*	Major	10
1.OA.D.8 Determine the unknown whole number in an addition or subtraction equation relating three whole numbers. *For example, determine the unknown number that makes the equation true in each of the equations 8 + ? = 11, 5 = □ − 3, 6 + 6 = □.*	Major	7
Number and Operations in Base Ten		
Extend the counting sequence.		
1.NBT.A.1 Count to 120, starting at any number less than 120. In this range, read and write numerals and represent a number of objects with a written numeral.	Major	18
Understand place value.		
1.NBT.B.2 Understand that the two digits of a two-digit number represent amounts of tens and ones. Understand the following as special cases:		
1.NBT.B.2a 10 can be thought of as a bundle of ten ones—called a "ten."	Major	12, 17, 21
1.NBT.B.2b The numbers from 11 to 19 are composed of a ten and one, two, three, four, five, six, seven, eight, or nine ones.		
1.NBT.B.2c The numbers 10, 20, 30, 40, 50, 60, 70, 80, 90 refer to one, two, three, four, five, six, seven, eight, or nine tens (and 0 ones).		
1.NBT.B.3 Compare two two-digit numbers based on meanings of the tens and ones digits, recording the results of comparisons with the symbols $>$, $=$, and $<$.	Major	22

The Standards for Mathematical Practice are integrated throughout the instructional lessons.

Common Core State Standards for Grade 1 Mathematical Standards	Content Emphasis	*Ready* Common Core Instruction Lesson(s)
Number and Operations in Base Ten *continued*		
Use place value understanding and properties of operations to add and subtract.		
1.NBT.C.4 Add within 100, including adding a two-digit number and a one-digit number, and adding a two-digit number and a multiple of 10, using concrete models or drawings and strategies based on place value, properties of operations, and/or the relationship between addition and subtraction; relate the strategy to a written method and explain the reasoning used. Understand that in adding two-digit numbers, one adds tens and tens, ones and ones; and sometimes it is necessary to compose a ten.	Major	23, 24, 25
1.NBT.C.5 Given a two-digit number, mentally find 10 more or 10 less than the number, without having to count; explain the reasoning used.	Major	19
1.NBT.C.6 Subtract multiples of 10 in the range 10-90 from multiples of 10 in the range 10-90 (positive or zero differences), using concrete models or drawings and strategies based on place value, properties of operations, and/or the relationship between addition and subtraction; relate the strategy to a written method and explain the reasoning used.	Major	20
Measurement and Data		
Measure lengths indirectly and by iterating length units.		
1.MD.A.1 Order three objects by length; compare the lengths of two objects indirectly by using a third object.	Major	31, 32
1.MD.A.2 Express the length of an object as a whole number of length units, by laying multiple copies of a shorter object (the length unit) end to end; understand that the length measurement of an object is the number of same-size length units that span it with no gaps or overlaps. *Limit to contexts where the object being measured is spanned by a whole number of length units with no gaps or overlaps.*	Major	33
Tell and write time.		
1.MD.B.3 Tell and write time in hours and half-hours using analog and digital clocks.	Supporting/ Additional	34
Represent and interpret data.		
1.MD.C.4 Organize, represent, and interpret data with up to three categories; ask and answer questions about the total number of data points, how many in each category, and how many more or less are in one category than in another.	Supporting/ Additional	29, 30

The Standards for Mathematical Practice are integrated throughout the instructional lessons.

Common Core State Standards for Grade 1 Mathematical Standards	Content Emphasis	*Ready* Common Core Instruction Lesson(s)
Geometry		
Reason with shapes and their attributes.		
1.G.A.1 Distinguish between defining attributes (e.g., triangles are closed and three-sided) versus non-defining attributes (e.g., color, orientation, overall size); build and draw shapes to possess defining attributes.	Supporting/ Additional	26
1.G.A.2 Compose two-dimensional shapes (rectangles, squares, trapezoids, triangles, half-circles, and quarter-circles) or three-dimensional shapes (cubes, right rectangular prisms, right circular cones, and right circular cylinders) to create a composite shape, and compose new shapes from the composite shape.	Supporting/ Additional	27
1.G.A.3 Partition circles and rectangles into two and four equal shares, describe the shares using the words *halves, fourths,* and *quarters,* and use the phrases *half of, fourth of,* and *quarter of.* Describe the whole as two of, or four of the shares. Understand for these examples that decomposing into more equal shares creates smaller shares.	Supporting/ Additional	28

Acknowledgments

Illustration Credits

page 26: Rob McClurkan

page 101: Rob McClurkan

page 195: Rob McClurkan

All other illustrations by Sam Valentino.